THE END OF THE RAINBOW

THE END OF THE RAINBOW

A P O T* of Gold for Everyone
*Personal Old-age Trust
*Prepaid One-time Tax

Introducing

The Social Trust Surety System

* A new way of retiring
* A new way of funding govenment
* A Social Security System that really is!
* Putting capitalism to work

by **Omer Nisley**
illustrated by **Penny Coffeen**

Published by
CPA Books
404 E. Ludlow
Rolling Prairie, IN 46371

Printed in the United States of America

ISBN 0-9659370-0-3

Library of Congress Catalog Card Number: 97-60961

CONTENTS
***

INTRODUCTION

"Work without hope draws nectar in a sieve,
And hope without an object cannot live."
Samuel T. Coleridge

There are many different ideas about what Social Security is. Some of these ideas are completely false. Others are only partially true. This book is meant to strip away some of the myths surrounding our Social Security System. It is a nasty job, but someone has to do it! After taking a realistic look at what Social Security is and is not, we will offer a radically new alternative to this institution which has served us very well for over 50 years.

No one really claims to understand Social Security. Benefits are not easily calculated as the formulas used to compute benefits are complex. Among those who intend to claim Social Security benefits, there is a lot of confusion and uncertainty. Misinformation abounds! This, coupled with an irrational fear that any changes to the system would spell disaster and threaten benefits, has crippled most efforts to reform the system!

Yet, Social Security has governed our behavior for several generations. Many people determine their retirement and much economic activity by their perceptions of what Social Security will do for them. The myths about the system to which we have subscribed have succeeded in derailing any real progress toward reforming this pervasive program! A whole generation of Americans has swallowed as "gospel" the half truths which their government and their peers have foisted upon them. Citizens of our country have wagered their financial well being on real or perceived fears. Old and outdated policies and practices remain unchallenged because of widespread ignorance. Unfortunately, what we don't understand, we fear and what we fear, we will not challenge unnecessarily!

There is hope, however! We can still transform not only the system, but the very way we prepare for retirement! We believe that properly understood and implemented, there can be a realistic Social Security System. But, we need one based on the capitalistic ideals which are the corner stones of our country's economic system. In the process of updating the Social Security system, we will find retirement ideas revolutionized. In addition, we believe there will be a radical

4

The End of the Rainbow

shift in the way our entire government is funded.

Literally thousands of years have passed since any basic changes have been made in governmental financing. Taxes are almost as old as human history. Taxing is easy, convenient and can be changed fairly easily as circumstances dictate. So why fix it if it isn't broke? Simply, because , while it may not be "broke" so many of us are! Taxes can be oppressive; they can stifle real economic growth; they can create some real hardships among the citizens. Taxes have always generated an undercurrent of resentment toward government. Would it not be wonderful if we could devise some other option!

Could there really be an alternative to income taxes? We believe there is! One which is much less painful, less confiscatory, more manageable and a lot more acceptable to the American public than our present way of collecting funds for Government operations! In the following pages you will find a simple idea applied to an old problem, with some exciting, almost unbelievable, results! We will explore with you a method of government support which is much less distressing than ever before! This new method, named by us

"The Social Trust Surety System" is easily instituted yet powerful and easily accepted.

This is more than just patching things up. It is a whole new way of looking at governmental financing. As you will discover, we will be able to have our cake and eat it, too!

Government Financing

"Just patch 'er up!"
We've never known anything else, so just repair it. Something new just couldn't be better!

SECTION I

Social

Security

Today

Chapter 1 **Prophet of Boom?**

*"Make no little plans; They have
no magic to stir men's blood."*
attributed to D. H. Burnham

Meet Mr. Joe Average. He is presently 24 years old, a factory worker making $24,000.00 per year. He is married with two children. Mr. Average was chosen to represent all of us, because his very modest income can serve as a benchmark for us. If Mr. Joe Average can make it, we can probably make it too!

Gloomy forecasts abound concerning Joe's economic future. What lies ahead for Mr. Average? What can he expect at 65, after working another 41 years? Can he actually retire at age 65? If he does, just what benefits can he expect from his government? Will Social Security be there for Mr. Average like it was for his parents?

A PEEK INTO THE FUTURE

With our computerized crystal ball, We will look in on Joe in the year 2035. This should be just five years before he is scheduled to retire. It is also 35 years from the time "The Plan" presented in this book was put into motion.

We are prepared for the worst! Poor Joe unquestionably faced a most uncertain future 35 years ago! The prospects of an aging population did not bode well for his economic health. His retirement expectations were never too optimistic! Back then, Joe was not sure that there would be any retirement benefits when his time came for that important time in his life. There were just too many people who were eligible for benefits and far too few workers predicted to pay for their entitlements!

SURPRISE!!

How interesting! Our crystal ball reveals a mystifying eye-opener! Mr. Joe Average seems to have done extremely well! Things look a lot different. But what is this?!!! Joe is already *retired*?!!! What radical twist of fate could have brought such a miracle about?

"Hey, Joe, we thought you had at least five more years to go before you could retire? What happened? Did you win the lottery?"

The End of the Rainbow

"Oh, no! I've retired on full pay! I've had the same job for 35 years and at the same salary. Now I'm ready to travel and enjoy life."

"Impossible! No one can really do that after working at your salary for 35 years, unless, of course, they've gone into politics!"

"Nothing of the kind!"

"Well then, maybe you had a rich uncle who left you a lot of money? No one can retire at full pay! At least, we have never heard of such a thing! You must have gotten your wealth somewhere!"

"Uncle Sam made it all possible! As a matter of fact, most workers in my age group have been able to retire after 35 years of work. They are doing it and still receiving retirement income equal to their full salary!"

"Uncle Sam made that possible? Be serious! The Uncle Sam we know could *never* provide for retirement at 60, or even at 65 or 70, especially at full salary! What's the catch?"

"There is no catch! Thirty-five years ago our lawmakers finally realized that something had change. The aging population was threatening to upset everything. A whole new generation of workers saw no way to retire with dignity unless radical changes were made to the system. This frustration turned out to be the catalyst to a totally new way of financing government. It was the first time that really long range planning was taken seriously by these elected officials. From its inception, Social Security was a political football! Politicians tried in many ways to patch up the old ways in the least offensive manner. Large and powerful groups always threatened anyone who dared hint of any changes that would affect their benefits!

No one really took the time to analyze and harness our capitalistic American foundations! We merely copied other world governments. We did what governments have done for thousands of years and raised money by collecting taxes. When the income from taxes was inadequate, we borrowed."

"What has all that got to do with you retiring at 60?"

"Everything! Now I am independently wealthy and have a guaranteed income for life. As a bonus, this plan has eliminated the Federal Income Tax! Fact is, although I actually pay less to the Government, I will contribute more financially than ever before! Our nation has paid off most of its debt, and we will soon be operating entirely in the black!

The End of the Rainbow

We are doing all this while phasing out personal income taxes entirely over the next several years!

"Excuse us, Joe. There must be something wrong with our crystal ball! What you are saying does not make much sense."

"It will when you begin to explore the power of compound interest! When our lawmakers began to harness this power 35 years ago, our whole understanding of social security was changed. We found that it changed our country in many other ways as well!"

TOO GOOD TO BE TRUE?

Does this look in the crystal ball sound too good to be true? Well, hang on! You are in for one of the most pleasant surprises of your life! The following pages will begin to unravel for you the truly astonishing power of invested money and how this dynamic principle can change the way we have done things for centuries!

This book will outline in broad powerful strokes the methods by which many ills can be addressed at last. Properly applied, we can recapture the American dream. We can promise all citizens, a truly financially secure retirement. In the process we can reaffirm our belief in the capitalistic philosophy which has always fueled our way of life. We will be able to practice what we preach, and do capitalism, even in government! While these claims may seem far beyond our reach, keep reading with an open mind. Digest the figures! It will slowly dawn on you that it is all possible! Not only is it possible, but it is deceptively easy to accomplish. We have been living with the answer under our noses for so long that we could not see it!

WHAT'S AHEAD?

You may wish to skip for now, the analysis of the present Social Security System. It is there so we can understand just how urgent our plight is! The old ways of doing business will simply not do any more! This may all be familiar to you, as many have explored the dilemmas we face.

You will want to read and reread this section once you have grasped the plan we are presenting. You will want to compare the obvious pitfalls of the "old" Social Security System with the "new" system outlined in Section II.

Section II covers the new plan and its many ramifications. We will share with you some of our best thinking about its details. We ask you to read Section II for the broad implications only. The details we describe may not be as important as the overall concept. They are not meant to be definitive or iron clad. You will surely think of other alternatives which would enhance and improve the central idea. If so, great! That is the purpose of this book! We need to get moving in the right direction before a whole generation of Americans misses out on all the wonderful opportunities our country offers.

Also, we will explore some of the profound changes this new concept will make on our society and government. We hope you will be absolutely astounded and then emboldened to work for the adoption of the Social Trust Surety System!

Section III will explore the rocky road of "getting there"! There are undoubtedly as many paths as there are serious thinkers. The important thing to remember is that we must begin now. We need to plan and implement SOME kind of program to get us there! We have shared our thinking in this section to illustrate that the goals are achievable! The task is far from impossible. The end result will be well worth any pain it takes to get there!

SOME ASSUMPTIONS

Economic Considerations

It is extremely difficult to work out all the future "what ifs". The statistics and financial data presented here are given as if there were no inflation phenomena to factor in. We know, however, that inflation will always be present. Our economic history is full of "cycles"! Realistically, there is no such thing as a totally "flat" economy.

Roaring inflation and crippling depression are a fact of economic life. All the stages between these two extremes are always a possibility. We will simply ignore them for our purposes. The ups and downs of our economy similarly affect the earnings of most investments. When the economy is robust, so usually are earnings. When the economy lags, earnings generally go down as well. Thus, the purchasing power of our investment earnings should stay fairly stable. This is not perfectly so, but close enough to make our point. The power of compound interest remains fairly constant, even if the intensity of that power varies!

It may even be that much greater economic stability may result from our plan than even we have anticipated.

*There will be a huge increase in the pool of investment money.

*There will be assured retirement income for everyone.

*The Federal Income Tax will be eliminated.

These will exert a negative pressure on inflation. The figures we use in this book, which are not inflation compensated, may well become the reality of the future! All this is covered in greater detail in subsequent chapters.

DEMOGRAPHIC CONSIDERATIONS

We know that our population is aging. All the statistics point to that conclusion. We will use the present figures, however, to judge our proposal. As you will see, this makes our figures extremely conservative. Under our plan, the more retired people we have in our population, the better the plan works! So we will analyze most data on the basis of today's statistics, including the mortality rate, knowing full well that these should change rather dramatically over the next 30 years.

Budget Considerations

We are assuming that the federal budget will remain at about the same level in purchasing power, enabling us to ignore the inflationary figures here as well.

We will also assume that with "The Plan" two very large budget items, social security payments and interest on the national debt, will be eliminated. Part of the national debt may still be with us in 35 years. Our program does not really begin to address the debt until the original "plan" enrollees begin to retire in approximately 35 years. Large budget cuts, however, will be possible as there will be fewer and fewer "entitlements" to drain it. But we will lay out our "picture" of the future as if all this had already been accomplished. As you will see, a debt free America will be possible within the lifetime of our younger generation! Our "crystal ball" should perhaps look 50 years into the future to be accurate!

OUR CHALLENGE

Have fun! What you are about to read should excite you. It will give you new hope for the future of America! You will catch a glimpse of the dawning of a brand new era for our great country.

The End of the Rainbow

Those of us who are too old to benefit from this new dream want sincerely to leave behind a legacy. Our children and grand children deserve something of lasting value from us. We inherited from the generation before us nothing but debts and ever higher taxes. Our parents made a noble effort to bring equality and economic stability to everyone. Their dream is still our dream, but the means must change. How this can be done we will explore in the following pages!

So, read and judge for yourself. The "plan" is so amazingly simple! yet, it promises all we have ever hoped for as Americans! Dare we hope that we can affect change before it is too late? Dream with me! Can catch the vision and work to make it come true! It can change everything.....and all for the better!

The plan is revolutionary. If we can break away from thousands of years of "tradition" and experiment with the ideas presented here, we will have an alternative way of financing government. The New Age has dawned and we can be a part of it!

In spite of the next section on Social Security's shortcomings, this book is not meant to be a prophet of gloom. On the other hand, we are offering one of the brightest hopes possible for our future generations! We propose a plan that offers a life free of income tax PLUS a relatively care free early retirement! We like to think we are the prophet of BOOM!

The Possible Dream!

The Social Trust Surety System makes retirement at full pay possible without the heavy burden of Income and Social Security taxes!

Chapter 2 **Ah, To Retire At Last!**

"It is with a pious fraud, as with a bad action;
it begets a calamitous necessity of going on."
Thomas Paine

Part of the American dream is to be able to retire and take life easy! We have this romance with the vision of a life of leisure. We look forward to the years when there will be time for travel and relaxation, without the constant daily pressure of "going to work".

If rest and relaxation are not your cup of tea, you have probably entertained the idea of being able to pursue a pet hobby, perhaps write a book or build your dream house in retirement! You might even look forward to volunteering your services to a church, hospital or community service organization. You will surely want time to be with and visit family and friends without the constraints of having to "get back to work"!

So enthralled are we with the retirement dream that millions play the lottery every day, hoping to be able to escape

21

the daily work regime and retire from their job. We want to get off the treadmill which robs us of the time to do what we really want to do!

While many of us truly enjoy working, we do, nevertheless, feel a deep seated desire to be economically independent. We really want to be totally free of "having" to go to work. Retirement promises us the freedom from being "chained" to a job.

One of the most destructive myths surrounding the present Social Security System is that Social Security will provide the income to make our retirement dream come true! But alas! The retirement we dream about will NEVER come to pass on just Social Security! The Social Security income projections are far short of being able to promise us financial independence!

DON'T TRY IT ON SOCIAL SECURITY INCOME!

SO, TAKE WARNING! THE RETIREMENT WE DREAM ABOUT WILL NEVER COME TO PASS ON SOCIAL SECURITY INCOME! To think otherwise is a myth which will lead you into a false security!

Calculations vary widely, based on many factors, but Mr. Joe Average can never expect income from Social Security to come anywhere close to his present meager yearly income. Based on Social Security alone he will take a big cut at retirement. The higher the yearly income has been, the greater becomes the disparity between what was being earned and what Social Security will pay!

Note that this is not the fault of Social Security! It was never meant to be the sole source of income for retirement! From the very first it was meant to be a "safety net". Congress created the Social Security System during the Great Depression. Its stated purpose was to assist workers who faced financial hardships caused by loss of wages during retirement. It was meant to *supplement* the retiree's own assets and resources.

During the Depression, many people lost everything. To live in retirement, they either had to work until the day they died, live in abject poverty, or depend upon relatives to sustain them. Social Security was devised to give such people a minimum amount for *survival*! It has always provided that kind of "survival" income for recipients.

But, Social Security cannot possibly provide the kind of income most of us require to live out our retirement fantasies. It will barely cover the cost of food and the most rudimentary kind of shelter! Forget travel; forget hobbies; forget the carefree life! None of these extras are possible, even with the most generous of Social Security retirement settlements!

Should illness strike, with all of its related expenses, or should circumstances require other emergency cash, Social Security retirement income alone will not reach! It was never meant to! It was meant to supplement, not support!

THE PERSISTENT MYTH

Yet the myth persists! Retire on Social Security? I've heard the expression thousands of times and I'm sure you have too! But it is a myth, pure and simple. Without some other assets or support there is only certain poverty at retirement! True, we won't starve, as long as there are no unforeseen financial crises or illnesses to rob us of our eating money! As millions of Americans have discovered, the prospect of growing old increasingly means an increasing level of uncertainty! Growing old almost always increases the risk of escalating medical expenses, further eroding our "Security" part of Social Security retirement income!

BUT WE'VE BASED OUR WHOLE LIFE ON IT!

Perhaps the most insidious part of this persistent myth is that we have had a whole generation of wage earners who have based their saving and spending habits on the myth! The psychological mind-set of this generation is *to spend* money, enjoy life, because retirement will be taken care of! We pay our Social Security for that day when we throw away the time card! Live life in the now! Buy all the goods your budget can afford, even borrowing if the payments are not too high!

The Rand research organization has concluded that very few Americans will be able retain their standard of living in retirement. The bottom 10 percent of white households with at least one spouse over 70 have an average of $765 in assets. The bottom 20 percent of blacks and the bottom 30 percent of Hispanics have NO household wealth!

What this means is that a large number of people have either not been able to or been unwilling to make provisions for living beyond their working years! Without any, or limited assets, as we have already seen, it should be possible to exist on Social Security, but *barely!* And only then, if unforeseen events do not siphon off even that meager income!

Economist James P. Smith of the Rand organization says, "Loud alarm bells are ringing for the future." And well they should be! Too many of us have swallowed the myth of retiring on Social Security alone!

The bleak results of this philosophy are well documented! Millions of workers retire, only to find out that their "dream" has vanished and they are faced with the stark reality of living life at or below the poverty level! Gone are the bright hopes of a government secured retirement income; gone are the dreams of travel and retirement pleasures; gone are the visions of a retirement free of financial worries!

WE DON'T EVEN SAVE ANY MORE!

The myth has destroyed the incentive to set aside money for that long awaited day of retirement. Social Security is simply not a savings program! It is a rather thinly veiled "conspiracy", where one generation promises the next one that if they are "good" and pay into the system for their "parents", they will be able to pull the same scam on their children!

A second myth, which many still cling to, despite warnings from everyone concerned, is that Social Security will be around for all time.

26

The End of the Rainbow

The Board of Trustees of the Social Security and Medicare Trust Funds report that the OASDI (Old Age Survivors and Disability Insurance) program will be able to continue paying benefits for the next 35 years, but are expected to be depleted under present law in the year 2030. According to the Trustees' 1995 report, the pay-roll tax contributions alone will not cover the full cost of promised benefits. From now until 2012 pay-roll deductions will pay for all benefits, but from 2012 until 2030 the funds will come from the accumulated trust fund's securities. By 2030 these will be all gone!   The Social Security Commissioner, Shirley S. Chater has stated that while we are not on the eve of a crisis, we must move forward....to discuss and debate the various proposals that will strengthen Social Security's long term solvency. This same report from the Boards of Trustees has their recommendation that an Advisory Council on Social Security "conduct an extensive review...(to) restore the long-range actuarial balance of the program."

While Social Security remains our most popular federal program, there has been increasing skepticism expressed over its ability to meet needs into the Twenty-first century. People are living longer than ever before. This puts a two-fold pressure on the present system. As retirees live longer, they will begin to withdraw on an average more and more over their lifetimes than they put into the system. This, coupled with the fact that there will be fewer and fewer workers paying into the system proportionately, means that some extremely crucial issues must be addressed if Social Security is to remain at even its present meager level of helpfulness!

THE TIME TO ACT IS NOW!

The time to do something is now. We must make certain that our children are not handed an expensive white elephant which will do nothing but deplete their resources and undermine their quality of life.

There have been numerous attempts to "fix" Social Security. The pay-roll deductions have steadily crept up over the years to meet the increasing demands made on the system. From all indications, employee\employer contributions will continue to go up! Fewer and fewer workers will be asked to support more and more retirees! Because so many of us actually believe in the myth that this "golden goose" of our generation can go on forever, there has been a tremendous resistance against any changes! "Don't mess with Social Security!" is a warning which some politicians have failed to

28

The End of the Rainbow

heed, often with dire consequences! The issue is a "hot potato" which just keeps on being tactfully and deliberately ignored by those who want to keep on getting elected! It is virtually impossible to talk about any meaningful changes without inflaming the passions of anyone over 50! Changes threaten anyone who perceives that THEIR BENEFITS would be adversely effected!

NO BENEFIT REDUCTIONS PLANNED!

Perhaps I should reassure you! The changes being proposed in this book will not CUT BENEFITS!! If you continue to read, you will discover that the new program, which we choose to call "The Social Trust Surety System" (an accurate description, but also a play on words to make it sound like a refinement of The Social Security System, which it is!), will cost less and yet be able to bring more benefits! This astounding contradiction will be explained in Section II!

There was a sign in a place of business I often frequented which reads, "A lack of planning on your part does not necessarily constitute an emergency on my part"! I can think of no better way to describe the current status of our Social Security System. We are most definitely in the "planning" stages. The "emergency" is clearly foreseen, but we can ignore it! It does not affect our generation. It is THEIR problem!

Let us leave something worthwhile to our children! Let us do some solid planning so that there will never be another "emergency" which threatens the whole "system"!

IT IS MY MONEY, ISN'T IT?

There is a third myth, which has already been alluded to and that is "Its my money!" It involves the whole issue of entitlements. We feel that we are entitled to "our money" which we have "paid into" the system.

Well, it's true, we HAVE been paying into the system all our lives. But have we really been building up equity? The answer is an unequivocal "NO"! All we have is "a strong and noble commitment by the generations who are currently working to pay for the retirement of those who are not, with the expectation that the generations to come will do the same when they retire." This is a quote from Senator Bob Kerrey of Nebraska as cited in the 1995 July-August issue of Modern Maturity. If you expect the system to keep on spitting out benefits, you must keep feeding contributions into it! There simply are no vast accumulated assets which we have built up which will result in benefits for us when we retire! The present way of doing business requires a healthy work force paying into the system when we are ready to collect benefits! We have not *prepaid* our retirement!

When we see this myth for what it is, we begin to realize just how badly we have saddled future generations with our own expectations. We expect to retire on the labors of future wage earners. If our parents were brazen enough to borrow their retirement from us, we should be able to do the same thing to our children! Long ago a prophet observed that "the fathers have eaten sour grapes and set the children's teeth on edge"! Why should our children have to pay for our negligence and lack of fiscal responsibility? Perhaps we can make up for the sins inflicted on us, by giving them something better! Stay tuned!

IT HASN'T BEEN ALL BAD!

Please note that our criticism of the system is in no way meant to detract from the great benefits which Social Security has brought to the American people! It has provided a much needed safety net for millions who would perhaps have starved without it. It has undoubtedly provided food and basic necessities to a countless hoard of needy people.

There was also the marvelous feature of Social Security which provided insurance to workers. Their dependents were assured that they would not be completely destitute in case of their untimely death. They also knew that Social Security would help them if they became disabled!

Our goal is not to trash the whole idea of Social Security! But we do want to look realistically at its obvious shortcomings. In this way we can perhaps find an even better way to achieve its lofty goals! We have come not to destroy Social Security, but to complete it!

KEY POINT to remember:

The "older" our population gets, the greater the pressure on our present system!

Social Security
as we know it

ORIGINALLY

The original concept of Social Security was the many affluent workers helping the unfortunate few.

TODAY
Presently, the younger work force is supporting the retired workers.

TOMORROW

In the future, fewer and fewer workers will support more and more retirees!

Chapter 3 **The Infernal Revenue Service**

"The marvel of all history is the patience with which men and women submit to burdens unnecessarily laid upon them by their governments."
Wm. H. Borah, speech in US Senate

None of us likes paying taxes. We complain about them constantly, but we recognize that like death, they are largely inevitable. In our most sober times, we grudgingly admit that we are performing a noble patriotic duty. We know that taxes are necessary to pay for the government we demand. And admittedly, over the years we have been demanding more and more from our government. Our collective demands have been outstripping our collective ability to pay! As a consequence we have built up a huge national debt!

Taxes have been with us from the earliest of recorded history! Taxes may have had their beginning as a voluntary contribution to the "tender of the fire" when everyone else got to "hunt" in cave man times. Someone had to look out for the clan's welfare in the absence of the "hunters"! Those whose "jobs" kept them from hunting, shared in the clan's bounty when they did return! This voluntary "sharing" with the clan "fire tenders" benefited everyone. This principle of sharing the bounty and the load is at the heart of government!

It was only a matter of time until voluntary contributions were replaced with a more rigid and compulsory system, and taxes were born! Everyone knew when a hunt started that a portion of the kill was going to go toward those who had to stay at home! It was only fair that the hunters "shared"!

So well has the system of taxation worked, that it has been with us for thousands of years! It is THE method of supporting government! Kings and kingdoms, governments of all description have come and gone, but taxes have remained! Up until the present, they have been as sure as death!

TAXES--A MIXED BLESSING

The power to tax has been a mixed blessing. When done fairly and with sensitivity everyone benefited. Programs and projects which would not have been possible any other way were possible when everyone shared in their cost.

36

The End of the Rainbow

Modern civilization would have been virtually impossible without taxes!

On the other hand, there have been governments whose power to tax has produced policies which were so oppressive that the citizens became virtual slaves.

Throughout history, taxes which were perceived as being unfair or oppressive have been the root cause of countless revolutions and rebellions! Our own United States was the direct result of a revolt against a government which the colonists perceived as one which exacted taxes, but returned little or nothing in exchange, except more oppression! "Taxation without representation is tyranny!" There are some today who would suggest that "taxation, even with representation, is tyranny"!

All governments, whether they were monarchies, democracies, or republics have used taxes to raise revenue. Taxes have been imposed by vote or decree and a multitude of variations in between. They have been paid willingly, through coercion, and sometimes by down right confiscation!

There are many many different kinds of taxes! Governments have been creative and prolific in creating ways to take money from the citizens. There are property taxes, based on the theory that if you can afford to own property, you should be able to afford to pay taxes. There have been income taxes, sales taxes, excise taxes, poll taxes, use taxes, and about as many others as the human mind was able to dream up. There have been taxes on automobiles, gasoline, telephone service, tobacco, alcohol, boats, planes and as many other goods and services as the human race has ever devised!

In some cases, especially in poor economic times, taxes can and often have become confiscatory. There have been cases when taxes were imposed which were impossible to pay. Some governments have seen fit to actually take property from its owners to pay the taxes it has imposed upon them.

Many of the taxes we pay are readily identifiable. Others are "hidden" and built into the cost of a service or goods. A simple truth about taxes: they affect everyone! Taxes ARE inevitable.

Yet, no one to our knowledge has ever come up with an alternative to taxes. UNTIL NOW that is! In Section II of this book we will explore a totally new way of funding government! It is so profoundly simple, we cannot help but wonder why it has never been used before. It may be because up to now we did not have computer technology to guide us! We have no excuses now! We have the tools to do better!

The End of the Rainbow

And we are going to explore HOW!

HOW MUCH IS ENOUGH?

So, just how much do we pay in taxes in our lifetime? We will explore the answer to this shortly. We must keep in mind that the actual amount paid may vary widely from one individual to another. The Federal Tax Laws have so many twists and turns in them that it becomes almost impossible to make accurate estimates. In general, you will pay more or less depending upon how many dependents you have, on where you get your income, on whether you are buying a home, and a host of other variables! But pay you will! Even with a modest income, you can expect to pay a small fortune to Uncle Sam during the course of your lifetime. The one tax most of us are very familiar with is the Federal Income Tax. It is this tax which we want to look at in more detail.

So, let's begin doing some quick calculations on how much we actually pay in Income Taxes. April 15 comes for all of us and that means the deadline for filing our Federal Income Taxes. If we are like the majority of U.S. citizens, we will wait until the last minute to make this dreaded calculation of our tax liability, especially if we know we will end up owing Uncle Sam money!

When Mr. Joe Average files his 1040 tax form, he will indicate that he has an income of $24,000. If he takes the standard deductions and has only himself and his wife as dependents, his tax bill for the year will be $1,916.00 at the 1994 rates.

If Joe continues to pay at this rate until he retires at 65-a total of 41 years- he will have paid into the Federal treasury a total of $78,556.00 in simple income tax.

NOW ADD SOCIAL SECURITY!

At the same time, Joe's Social Security payments will be 7.65% of his income, or $1836.00 per year. Using the same facts as above, he would pay into the System a total of $75,276! The often overlooked fact is that his employer will **also** be paying into the System to the tune of $75,276!

Some may argue that Joe does not really pay the employer's portion of his Social Security payments. While this is technically true, it is wrong to overlook it. If the employer did not have to pay this tax for Joe, it could very well have been able to pay that amount directly to Joe, or at least provide other benefits to him which equalled this amount. In the end, it is really **Joe** who winds up paying! Over a lifetime

The End of the Rainbow

Joe will pay to his government, approximately $230,000 in taxes!

It will be important for us to remember these figures. We will be referring to them again when we look at the tax burden for Joe under the New Social Security System (which we have renamed the Social Trust Surety System). Joe's share of income tax is approximately $79,000 and his "share" for Social Security is approximately $150,000! Note that if Joe takes advantage of the many tax breaks afforded him throughout his working years, his tax "bill" could be considerably less. Having children, and buying a house with a mortgage, for example, are but two very probable ways Joe will save on his tax bill. A fair estimate of Joe's lifetime tax bill to the Federal Government is that it should be close to $200,000. If we discount the employer's share of his Social Security, Joe's personal contribution is closer to $125,000 --A remarkable figure for someone who only makes $24,000 per year!

WHERE DOES TAX MONEY COME FROM?

Personal income taxes, like Joe's, were the source of 35% of the money paid into the Federal treasury. In 1992 this amounted to $476 billion! Social Security, on the other hand, contributed 30% of the budget income, or a total of $413.7 billion. Combined, these two sources account for fully 65% of the Government's operating funds! Miscellaneous taxes (at 7%) and Corporate Income taxes (at 7%) round out the actual income. Note that at present, an astounding 21% of the budget was covered by borrowing!

WHERE DOES IT GO?

On the expenditure side, it is apparent that by far the largest budget outlay was for Social Security payments, Medicare and other retirement programs! This amounts to $469.7 billion (1992 figures). As we will see in Section II, almost all of this expenditure will be eliminated under the new Social Trust Surety System! Just think, 33% of our National Budget eliminated in 35 years! We will soon explore how this will be made possible.

The second largest budget outlay is for National Defense and all its related programs. This includes economic assistance to foreign countries. Our new approach to Government financing does nothing to this portion of the Budget. We will need to assume that the $348.6 billion allocated to Defense will remain at approximately this level.

Social programs are the third largest item at $235.6 billion, or 17% of the total budget. It is our observation and guess that many of these programs can and will be at least partially scaled back. But let us assume that there will be no changes and that we will keep the spending at or near the present levels.

WHAT ABOUT THE NATIONAL DEBT?

Interest on the National Debt consumes 14% of our Budget dollars. $199.4 billion were spent in 1992 on interest alone! Under our proposal this expenditure could be almost completely eliminated! We should be able to eliminate the National Debt entirely and operate a balanced budget under the new plan!

Interest on the National Debt, taken together with the Social Security payments, is a grand total of 47% of the Federal Budget. We have projected that not only would these two items be eliminated using the Social Trust Surety System, but that Federal Income would actually rise! Can you imagine some of the truly marvelous results of such a scenario? Can you imagine the highways and high speed rail systems which could be built. Can you imagine the research and development which could take place? Can you visualize free education for all who want it? Note that this is all possible!

This may be a good time to look briefly at the National Debt. In 1995 the National Debt was $4.7 trillion! This is approximately 3 times the Federal Budget, which stands at approximately $1.2 trillion. It is hard for most of us to comprehend figures this large. Somewhat easier to understand is that the National Debt is approaching $15,000 for each man, woman and child in America today! The truly sad part is that it continues to grow at an alarming rate. We are simply spending more money for government than we are able or willing to pay in taxes. As a consequence, we are leaving our children a legacy of debt and potential fiscal ruin!

We have added these statistics so that the full impact of our new Social Trust Surety System can be properly assessed. By completely eliminating Social Security payments and then reducing the interest we pay on the National Debt, we should be able to balance the budget AND pay off the debt entirely!

The End of the Rainbow

SOME MORE PROMISES!

In the next section of our book, we will explore how this will all become possible IF WE TAKE STEPS NOW TO MAKE IT HAPPEN! I really don't blame you if you are skeptical at this point. When I began to explore ways to "fix" the conditions described above, I had no idea that such simple changes could have such profound effects! Yet the effects are truly revolutionary. We really can have carefree and productive retirement AND we can have a lifetime free of PERSONAL INCOME TAX! So, read on!

Death and Taxes

SECTION II

A

REVOLUTIONARY

PROPOSAL

A "P O T" of Gold for Everyone!

Chapter 4 **Taking an Interest in Interest**

*"If you want to know whether you are destined to be a
success or a failure in life, you can easily find out.
The test is simple and it is infallible. Are you able
to save money? If not, drop out. You will lose."*
James J. Hill

Before we actually lay out the details of the new Social
Trust Surety System there is one basic principle we must
understand. The Social Trust Surety System is based on the
explosive power of compound interest!

Because we have largely been a nation of consumers,
we have not generally given much attention to the earning
potential of savings. Much of our economic energy is spent in
trying to figure out what our payments would be on a new
purchase. We do a lot of calculating about payments for a
new car, a boat or a house, but devote very little effort to
discovering the dynamics of saving!

We vaguely realize that making purchases "on time"
ends up costing us more money. We further realize that the

49

convenience of "buy now pay later" means that interest will be added to our payments. Just how much extra this adds to the price tag is not really important to us, as long as the monthly payments are within our ability to pay! We evaluate purchases on the basis of the size of the installment payment necessary, not in the total cash outlay of principal and interest.

We realize, somewhere in the deep recesses of our minds, that interest is one of the prices we pay to own something. Rarely do we consider interest as a possible source of income! Mortgages and installment payments are as American as apple pie!

Of course, it is almost impossible for an average American to buy a house without a mortgage. Paying interest and building up equity in a home is still far superior to paying rent and ending up with nothing! But we do pay for the privilege of buying a house for our family without cash or assets to do so. This means that someone is getting our interest money! How would you like to be on the receiving end of this interest?

What many of us do not understand in our credit culture is the awesome power of investing! We have all but forgotten that we can EARN interest as well as PAY it. When we add to this power of interest the added feature of earning interest on the interest we can really get excited! This feature, which we call compound interest makes some truly miraculous things happen! If you are among those of us who have never really looked at how money can earn money, you are in for some exciting surprises!

EARN SOME BIG BUCKS!

Let's begin by playing a little mind game. You have a chance to go to work for a very generous employer who offers you your choice of compensation packages. You will only be working for 30 days and once you choose an option, you will not be able to change your mind.

The first form of compensation is very straight forward. You earn $10,000.00 per day. (I told you the employer was very generous!) This means that at the end of 30 days you will receive a grand total of $300,000.00! Not bad for a month's work!

The second compensation package is very different. You must agree to work the first day for one cent. The second day and each day after that you will double the previous day's wages. This means that you will earn two cents the second day, four cents the third, etc.

Money Bags Employer

	Method 1 *Per Day Pay*				Method 2 *Double Every Day*	
	Per Day	Total			Per Day	Accumulated
1	$10,000.00	10,000.00			.01	.01
2	$10,000.00	20,000.00			.02	.03
3	$10,000.00	30,000.00			.04	.07
4	$10,000.00	40,000.00			.08	.15
5	$10,000.00	50,000.00			.16	.31
6	$10,000.00	60,000.00			.32	.63
7	$10,000.00	70,000.00			.64	1.27
8	$10,000.00	80,000.00			1.28	2.55
9	$10,000.00	90,000.00			2.56	5.11
10	$10,000.00	100,000.00			5.12	10.23
11	$10,000.00	110,000.00			10.24	20.47
12	$10,000.00	120,000.00			20.48	40.95
13	$10,000.00	130,000.00			40.96	81.91
14	$10,000.00	140,000.00			81.92	163.83
15	$10,000.00	150,000.00			163.84	327.67
16	$10,000.00	160,000.00			327.68	655.35
17	$10,000.00	170,000.00			655.36	1,310.71
18	$10,000.00	180,000.00			1,310.72	2,621.43
19	$10,000.00	190,000.00			2,621.44	5,242.87
20	$10,000.00	200,000.00			5,242.88	10,485.75
21	$10,000.00	210,000.00			10,485.76	20,971.51
22	$10,000.00	220,000.00			20,971.52	41,943.03
23	$10,000.00	230,000.00			41,943.04	83,886.07
24	$10,000.00	240,000.00			83,886.08	167,772.15
25	$10,000.00	250,000.00			167,772.16	335,544.31
26	$10,000.00	260,000.00			335,544.32	671,088.63
27	$10,000.00	270,000.00			671,088.64	1,342,177.27
28	$10,000.00	280,000.00			1,342,177.28	2,684,354.55
29	$10,000.00	290,000.00			2,684,354.56	5,368,709.11
30	$10,000.00	300,000.00			5,368,709.12	10,737,418.23
T		$300,000.00				10,737,418.23

52

Does not sound very promising, does it? Sure enough, the first 15 days of this plan do not pay very well. Even by the 20th day your wages for the day are far below the $10,000 per day the first plan offers.

So, how did you do? Look at the chart on page 52. You will discover that on the 30th day of plan 2 you will earn an unbelievable $5,368,709.12! The 30 day total is well over $10 million! Not bad for 30 day's work!

THE AWESOME POWER OF COMPOUNDING

How can this possibly be? Grasp this awesome power of doubling and you will begin to understand the power of compounding! It is this power which drives our new Social Trust Surety System. It will never turn a penny into millions; there are not enough doubling time units to do this. The power of compounding will, however, turn some rather modest investments into an impressive total!

Another way of looking at compound interest is to observe what happens to $1,000.00 invested and left to accumulate interest at 7.5%.

Let's just say that Mr. Joe Average takes $1,000.00 at

53

age 20 and invests in an enterprise which earns him 7.5%. Many modern investment vehicles which have the freedom to buy and sell stocks and bonds and get into and out of the money markets have done consistently better than that! Most well managed funds are capable of giving Joe a 7.5% return over and above the inflation rate.

What will Joe's $1000.00 be worth at age 65? Let's look at the charts. In 45 years when Joe is 65, his original $1000 will be worth almost $25,000.00! In just 45 years the accumulated interest and the interest on the interest have grown his nest egg to over 25 times the original sum!

Had Joe been able to start with a larger investment or if he had been able to earn a higher rate of return, compound interest would have made him rich!

SOME LESSONS

There are several lessons in this compound interest story. The first is obvious. The higher the interest rate the faster your money will grow! We know from the above that doubling your money is the key which gives compound interest its power.

The End of the Rainbow

INVEST $1,000 at 7.5% Compounded Annually

year	Balance	Int		year	Balance	Int
1	$1,075.00	75.00		24	$5,672.87	$395.78
2	1,155.63	80.63		25	6,096.34	425.47
3	1,242.30	86.67		26	6,555.72	457.38
4	1,335.47	93.17		27	7,047.39	491.68
5	1,435.63	100.16		28	7,575.95	528.55
6	1,543.30	107.67		29	8,144.14	568.20
7	1,659.05	115.75		30	8,754.96	610.81
8	1,783.48	124.43		31	9,411.58	656.62
9	1,917.24	133.76		32	10,117.45	705.87
10	2,061.03	143.79		33	10,876.25	758.81
11	2,215.61	154.58		34	11,691.97	815.72
12	2,381.76	166.17		35	12,568.87	876.90
13	2,560.41	178.63		36	13,511.54	942.67
14	2,752.44	192.03		37	14,524.90	1,013.37
15	2,958.88	206.43		38	15,614.27	1,089.37
16	3,180.79	221.92		39	16,785.34	1,171.07
17	3,419.35	238.56		40	18,044.24	1,258.90
18	3,675.80	256.45		41	19,397.56	1,353.32
19	3,951.49	275.69		42	20,852.37	1,454.82
20	4,247.85	296.36		43	22,416.30	1,563.93
21	4,566.44	318.59		44	24,097.52	1,681.22
22	4,908.92	342.48		45	25,904.84	1,807.31
23	5,277.09	368.17		46	27,847.40	1,942.86

Bankers and investors have used what they call "the rule of 72" for years. With the rule of 72, we can quickly calculate how often an investment will double at any given interest rate. The "rule of 72" works like this:

The interest rate is divided into 72. The answer is the number of years (or a very close approximation) it will take for an investment to double. For example, if the interest rate is 7.2%, it would take 10 years for doubling. This means that at 7.2%, Joe's $1000 would be worth $2000 in 10 years. In another 10 years it would be worth $4000. In 30 years, after doubling 3 times, the investment is valued at $8,000.00 and in 40 years at $16,000.00.

Now let's pretend that Joe finds a place to put his original $1000 which pays him an annual interest of 14.4%, just two times the above example. Now the investment doubles every 5 years (72 divided by 14.4). Now Joe will have doubled his investment 4 times in 20 years! This means that he will have $16,000.00 from his original $1000.

Note the power of that doubling. In 25 years (another doubling) he will have $32,000.00; in 30- $64,000; in 35- $128,000; and in 40 years, $256,000.00! In 50 years Joe's original investment of $1000 would be worth over $1 million at 14.4% interest compounded annually! Do you believe that money can work for you!!

It is obvious, however, that Joe is more interested in the safety of his $1000 than in having it work for him. If he merely tucks the money into his mattress or hides it in a safe deposit box, he can know that he will have his $1000!

BE SAFE OR EARN MORE?

One of the rules of investing is that generally the safer an investment is, the lower the return. The opposite is also generally true. The higher the return on investment the greater is the risk.

Had Joe been persuaded to place his $1000 in a pass book savings account at his local bank, we know that it would be safe!

We also know that Joe would be lucky to earn half of his 7.5% goal. But at 3.6%, we know from the rule of 72 that his money would double every 20 years. Now Joe could expect his $1000 to be worth $2000 in 20 years and $4,000.00 at the end of 40 years. If we did not know the power of compound interest, we would think this was a good deal! But now, Joe wants better! He is going to look for the highest possible return which affords him the greatest degree of safety possible.

Look at what a difference varying rates of return can give Joe:

at 3.6%   *$1000 will be worth* **$4000** *in 40 years.*

at 7.2%   *$1000 will be worth* **$16,000** *in 40 years.*

at 14.4% *$1000 will be work* **$256,000** *in 40 years*!

While Joe wants to keep his risk exposure as low as he can, he is also looking for the highest rate of return. Regardless of how he decides to invest, he will want to make his money work for him. Properly done, that money will work harder for him than he could possibly work for himself! Making money work for us by utilizing compound interest is at the heart of our Social Trust Surety System. The first rule is: *INVEST AT THE HIGHEST RATE OF RETURN COMPATIBLE WITH THE RISK FACTORS YOU ARE WILLING TO TAKE.*

SAVE WHEN YOU ARE YOUNG!

A second rule in investing is very apparent from the above: *START EARLY*! The longer an investment is left to work for you, the more often is has a chance to double! Even modest sums invested early in life can turn out to be real winners in later years!

There is an old Pennsylvania Dutch saying, "We get too soon old and too late smart." What a shame that so many of our generation have to "get too late smart"! The time to invest is long past for those of us ready to retire. We can only look back and see "what could have been"!

The Social Trust Surety System makes sure that this never happens again to any generation! It makes sure that money is put away to work its magic from the very first working years! No more the lure of buy now, pay later! Now the cry should be INVEST EARLY AND REAP THE HARVEST IN LATER YEARS!

INVEST AS MUCH AS YOU CAN!

The Third Rule is: Invest all you can! It is fairly obvious that the more you put aside, the more you will have working for you! We know if $1000 can bring Joe $16,000 at the end of 40 years, $2000 will bring him $32,000!

With this in mind, it is our advice to set aside as much money as you can *AND CONTINUE DOING SO YEAR*

AFTER YEAR! Doing this will put your money to work----
so you won't have to later on!

NOW WE CAN GO ON!

Now that you have seen the wondrous possibilities of
investing and of earning compound interest, we can go on. If
you truly understand the awesome power in this investment
concept, you will readily understand our proposed Social
Trust Surety System!

REMEMBER:

      *Save early and often

      *Invest at the highest rate of return at a

        tolerable risk

      *Save ALL you can

AND TIME WILL MAKE YOU RICH!!

Interest
The
Money
Machine

INTEREST

Watch the money grow!

Chapter 5 **The Social Trust Surety System**

"Put not your trust in money, but put your money in trust."
Oliver Wendell Holmes

The idea for the Social Trust Surety System came out of a study of alternatives to our present Social Security System. I started by playing with different investment strategies. I had a great computer spreadsheet program and played a number of "what if" games! The conclusions I reached from these "games" were so startling that I just had to check again to make sure there was not some mistake!

There have been a number of books and articles written outlining the wonderful magic of compound interest. If you have not already done so, please review the previous chapter to give you at least a nodding acquaintance with this concept.

We chose an investment return of 7.5% for all our calculations. There have been studies which have indicated that an even higher return (in real, not inflationary, numbers) would not be unreasonable to expect. Most quality investment funds which are free to use stocks, bonds, treasury bonds, etc. freely, have done considerably better over the past 20 years. This makes our calculations very conservative!

So, at 7.5%, how much would Mr. Joe Average have to save per year and for how long to give him a yearly return equal to or better than his present salary? Remember, the 7.5% average yearly earnings figure is conservative!

The following computer print-out shows the surprising results. If Mr. Joe average earns $24,000 per year (and the actual amount whether higher or lower yields the same relative result), he needs to invest 10%, or in his case $2,400 per year for 35 years. In 35 years his annual earnings on his savings is approximately equal to his annual salary!

This means that, all other things being equal, Joe could retire at the end of 35 years and continue to receive $24,000 per year for as long as he lives! He would never have to touch the principal. The earnings alone would be enough to give Mr. Average his full retirement income. Even if Joe lived to be 110, his annual income would never decrease. (See chart on next page)

The End of the Rainbow

Joe's Retirement Plan
(Investments at 7.5%)

Yr	Contributions	Interest	Balance
1	$ 2,400.00	0.00	2400.00
2	$ 2,400.00	180.00	4980.00
3	$ 2,400.00	374.00	7754.00
4	$ 2,400.00	582.00	10,735.00
5	$ 2,400.00	805.00	13,940.00
6	$ 2,400.00	1,046.00	17,386.00
7	$ 2,400.00	1,304.00	21,090.00
8	$ 2,400.00	1,582.00	25,071.00
9	$ 2,400.00	1,880.00	29,352.00
10	$ 2,400.00	2,201.00	33,953.00
11	$ 2,400.00	2,546.00	38,8990.00
12	$ 2,400.00	2,917.00	44,217.00
13	$ 2,400.00	3,316.00	49,933.00
14	$ 2,400.00	3,745.00	56,078.00
15	$ 2,400.00	4,206.00	62,684.00
16	$ 2,400.00	4,701.00	69,785.00
17	$ 2,400.00	5,234.00	77,419.00
18	$ 2,400.00	5,806.00	85,626.00
19	$ 2,400.00	6,422.00	94,448.00
20	$ 2,400.00	7,084.00	103,931.00
21	$ 2,400.00	7,795.00	114,126.00
22	$ 2,400.00	8,559.00	125,086.00
23	$ 2,400.00	9,381.00	136,867.00
24	$ 2,400.00	10,265.00	149,532.00
25	$ 2,400.00	11,215.00	163,147.00
26	$ 2,400.00	12,236.00	177,783.00
27	$ 2,400.00	13,334.00	193,517.00
28	$ 2,400.00	14,514.00	210,430.00
29	$ 2,400.00	15,782.00	228,613.00
30	$ 2,400.00	17,146.00	248,159.00
31	$ 2,400.00	18,612.00	269,170.00
32	$ 2,400.00	20,188.00	291,758.00
33	$ 2,400.00	21,882.00	316,040.00
34	$ 2,400.00	23,703.00	342,143.00
35	$ 2,400.00	**25,661.00**	**$370,204.00**

NOW COMPARE THAT WITH THE PRESENT SYSTEM!

Compare this with Joe's present Social Security prospects! Let's pretend that Social Security will survive until Joe reaches retirement age. Note that under the present laws the retirement age has been moved back, and Joe must wait until he is 67 to be eligible for full benefits! At the present rate, Joe's individual retirement benefit would be set at approximately $800 per month. The rate under the new STSS, based on our earnings as indicated in the Chart, would be around $2,000 per month! The two different plans are not even close! Joe's income from his Social Trust Surety System are 2 and one half (2 1/2) times more that his projected benefits from Social Security.

Not only could Joe retire at age 60 under STSS, but his monthly income would be much higher. Is there any question about which plan Joe would choose if he had a choice? It does not take a genius to see the obvious improvements STSS makes to Joe's quality of life as he faces his retirement years!

THERE IS EVEN MORE!

But the story is not yet over! We are going to see how this unique savings for retirement can actually do away with the Personal Income Tax! First, lets explore how Joe is going to put aside $2,400 per year (or 10%) on his meager salary.

In Chapter 3 we noted that Joe was paying over $1,800 per year in Social Security taxes alone. We pointed out that his employer was also paying over $1,800 into the Social Security System! From Joe's earnings, the Social Security System was receiving a grand total of over $3,600 per year (half from Joe, half from Joe's employer).

Under STSS, Joe would be responsible for putting $2,400 a year into his POT (Personal Old-Age Trust). The "system" would not care where that $2,400 came from! Joe and his employer may agree to both pay a portion. If each paid one-half, or $1,200 per year, both would still get off cheaper than under the "old" Social Security System! We can see how many employers might want to add to the benefits package offered to their employees by promising to pay all or part of the POT contributions.

Consider also that Joe will no longer be paying personal Income Taxes under STSS. His total outlay for what is now Social Security and Income Taxes is a mere 10% of his earnings! This assumes that his employer does not help him at all with his POT.

So now we have Joe and\or his employer putting 10% of Joe's earnings into a Personal Old-age Trust. This POT would be an investment fund, (a Trust, if you will) approved by the STSS. Joe would never be able to claim any portion of the assets of his POT, but it would be the source of his earnings during retirement!

Should Joe wish to, he could contribute MORE that 10% to his POT and retire even earlier. Note what happens if both Joe and his employer continue to contribute to Joe's POT at approximately 15% (or 7.5% each). Now Joe would be able to retire after 30 years! If he started to work at age 20, he could retire when he was 50 and continue receiving earnings until he died!

Under our original concept, Joe would ALWAYS contribute 10% of whatever he earned to his POT. If he continues to work after retirement, 10% of those earnings will always go into the POT.

PAYING FOR THE "INSURANCE"

Earnings withdrawn from his POT would also be "taxed" at the 10% rate. But there is a difference in WHERE this EARNINGS TAX goes. In STSS the 10% would go toward INSURANCE for the non-retirement age disabled workers and the dependents of workers who died before they were able to retire. As we will see later there should be more than enough "Insurance" money to cover disability and survivors payments.

So far we have determined some very important aspects of our new Social Trust Surety System. We will uncover more later!

1.   First, **STSS is far cheaper** that Social Security! STSS takes 10% of Joe's earnings. Social Security takes from Joe and his employer over 15%. By cooperating, both can save money! Should Joe have to pay the full 10% by himself, his employer could theoretically pay him higher wages, because they would have no more matching Social Security Funds to pay! In either case, Mr. Joe Average should be better off financially with STSS.

2.   Secondly, **STSS promises more benefits!** Joe would be able to retire EARLIER and receive higher monthly income from his POT than he ever would under even the most liberal projections with Social Security. (We will cover the Insurance aspect of Social Security in the next Chapter.) Suffice it to say that Joe is still covered in case he becomes disabled or dies prematurely during his working years!

Please note that Joe's POT never diminishes! It only has the potential to grow larger. The principal is never touched. Joe is able to draw only EARNINGS from his POT. We shall see in the next chapter why that will be the rule.

Retirement --
a Blessing or a Curse?

Depends a lot on whether

-your money works for you or   -you work for your money !

Chapter 6 **What Happens to the POT?**

"It is not necessary that a man should earn his living by the sweat of his brow unless he sweats easier than I do."

Thoreau

As you can tell from the previous charts, Joe's POT (Personal Old-age Trust) has accumulated almost one-third of a million dollars for his retirement! Not bad, considering Joe's very modest $24,000 annual income!

But now we are going to add another twist to this very valuable asset. To do so, we will place some important restrictions on Joe's POT and make it a real "trust" fund! Joe will not "own" his POT, he will be the "trustee" only. His only rights as trustee is to withdraw EARNINGS from his POT at his retirement!

Remember, Joe's contributions to his POT are mandatory. Every time Joe earns any money (outside of his POT withdrawals), he MUST contribute 10% of it to his POT. We feel that the time will come, when this system is fully

71

operational, that a number of exceptions might apply, especially after Joe reaches retirement status. Such things as profits on the sale of a home, or on capital gains, may eventually be treated very kindly to encourage even more savings by the public, which is the key to our new economics!

So, Joe and his employer, if he is so moved, will make regular contributions to Joe's POT based on 10% of his earnings. This will pose no serious problems and is a much lighter "tax" on Joe's earnings than his present personal income tax! Payroll deductions for this 10% contribution will be made and noted on Joe's year-end statement of earnings (W-2 form). It is a routine very familiar to us! This accounting will be important so that Joe Average, his employer, and the government will all know the status of the Trust Account in Joe's name.

This 10% contribution of EARNINGS will always be a part of the STSS program. Any citizen receiving money from any source will be asked to contribute 10% of it to their POT for as long as they live. Every citizen, regardless of age, will have their own POT and will be required to contribute to it, just as they were obligated to pay Personal Income Taxes under the "old" system.

While we do not make any predictions, we do not

72

The End of the Rainbow

foresee a mandatory retirement age. Joe will be free to work until the day he dies, IF HE SO CHOOSES. He would also be free to choose to retire the moment his POT earnings become large enough to support him at the level he chooses to be supported! If his POT EARNS enough to satisfy his self determined needs and desires, Joe will be allowed to retire! But, beware! Joe will NEVER be allowed to touch the principal of his POT! And if he decides to work later on, 10% of any earned income must go into the POT principal! We can foresee that some restrictions might apply later on relating to the MINIMUM age Joe could start withdrawing earnings. This is to ensure that the POT principal has a chance to grow.

WHAT ABOUT INSURANCE?

One of the issues we have not addressed is what to do if a worker dies prematurely or is disabled. Many have argued (and with good cause) in favor of the present Social Security System on exactly this issue. Advocates say that while the "return" on investment in Social Security is not all that great, the value of the insurance it provides more than offsets that deficiency. Being able to receive an income should you ever become disabled or know that your family will be provided for in case of your untimely death, is one of the strongest attractions of the present system.

So how will STSS provide for this kind of insurance? Is Joe to merely take his chances? We all realize how very important such insurance is! It is not be left to chance! The risk is just too great!

Rick Foster, who is the Social Security Administration's Deputy Chief Actuary, has stated that between the ages of 20 to 65 (normal working years), a worker faces a 2-in-10 possibility of dying and a 3-in-10 chance of becoming disabled! The odds are much too high to risk going through our working years without some kind of insurance. We want to know that we and/or our dependents will not become destitute should premature death or disability strike us!

KEEP ON CONTRIBUTING!

We propose that under STSS the 10% contributions continue, even after a worker taps into his POT for retirement income. THIS 10% tax from POT earnings, however, goes into an insurance fund! The insurance fund, supported by all retirees, is used to cover payments to disabled workers and to

The End of the Rainbow

surviving dependents, just like Social Security does now. We feel, from studying the statistics, that the actual level of support benefits will be much greater to these victims of misfortune than is possible now under the Social Security Administration!

While the calculations are somewhat muddled, because totally accurate statistics are not readily available, we can think our way through them. Let's examine premature death, for example.

If a worker dies with an infant dependant, the longest payout on behalf of that dependent is 21 years. There will be, of course, exceptions to this (an unborn infant for example or a disabled child), but 21 years is a reasonably accurate estimate of the *maximum* number of years the insurance must pay out. From experience we know that the actual AVERAGE will be much less than this!

The fair thing to do, if Joe dies prematurely, is to continue to pay his family Joe's full salary! This means, in his case, that $24,000.00 will be paid to Joe's widow until his children reach adulthood (21 years old). Note that this $24,000 is paid to Joe's widow. She counts this as income and is, therefore, required to put 10% of it into HER POT. This is insurance *income* for her, not "retirement income from

POT earnings" and must, by our definition, be "tithed". If she chooses to work at any time, her earnings are also "taxed" at 10% and put into her POT. This means that she will be able to begin withdrawing from HER POT after 35 years and Joe's original POT goes to pay his life-time taxes!

You may be wondering at this point why we must always put in 10% of our earnings into the POT, even after we retire or while receiving other benefits? The answer is very simple. There is another definition of POT. It can also stand for Prepaid One-time Tax! You see, there are NO INCOME TAXES as such under the Social Trust Surety System! You will, however, always pay the 10% of all earnings into a TRUST account from which YOU or your DEPENDENTS benefit for the rest of your life.

When you die, after having lived your retirement years from the POT earnings, this TRUST becomes your LIFETIME payment of your governmental obligations! The POT goes, in its entirety, to pay your ONE TIME income tax! There is no other income tax to pay during your entire life!

NO INCOME TAX!!

Yes, you heard right! No income tax during your

The End of the Rainbow

entire life! How can this be? Is the government deprived? NOT AT ALL! Let's look at some statistics.

First of all, Joe's Personal Income Tax was originally estimated to be just under $80,000 for a lifetime of work. The amount would even be less if Joe had more children, had high deductible medical costs, gave generously to charity or had paid a great deal of interest on his mortgage. The $80,000 is considered a maximum amount, and it could be a lot less!

Joe also contributes to the Social Security Administration all during his working years, but, because he also plans to make claims on it and from it, we shall not consider this to be a part of his contribution to Governmental support!

Under the Social Trust Surety System, Joe's contribution to his government will be over $350,000.00! This is at least 4 times more than he would have paid under the old system! We will be speculating in the next chapter what this might mean for our nation. Needless to say, Joe's contribution and the contributions of his fellow Americans will be greatly expanded, not from actual contributions, but from interest earned from his POT! This should enable America to regain much of its economic edge and allow the generations growing up in the next century to regain much of the "quality of life" we have lost in the most recent years of our history! There should be more money than ever for Government services--at least 4 times more! We will explore what this might mean in a later chapter.

Now we must admit, Joe's contributions are really modest compared to those who make a lot more than he does. We can assume for our calculations that $350,000 is a "fair" or average share of every American worker's contribution to their government's operations. It does not take a rocket scientist to figure out that if every citizen contributes four times more to their government than they once did, wonderful things can happen. We can foresee a time when State and local governments can share in this newly found wealth-- and taxes as we presently know them will be obsolete!

Note also that Joe's own POT has saved the government from paying out any Social Security benefits, presently estimated to be fully 33% of the Federal Budget! So our Social Trust Surety System is putting more dollars into the federal treasury (by a factor of 4!) and at the same time cutting expenses by one-third! The actual amount will be more like 50% savings as ALL retirement payments from the Federal Budget come closer to that figure!

This means that the actual reduction in the Federal Budget

expenses is approximately 50%! The national debt would be eliminated after only a few short years! Note that a 50% reduction in the Budget with a 400% increase in income makes for a very powerful and RICH Federal Government.

HOW MUCH WILL DISABILITY COST THE SYSTEM?

Now let's see what insurance we may need for the disabled. Remember, Mr. Foster predicted that 3-in-10 workers between 20 and 65 would become disabled before retirement. While accurate figures are not available, we will assume that fully 1/2 or more of these become disabled in the 10 years just prior to their retirement. This means that under the Social Trust Surety System, one-half of the newly disabled **will already be living off their POT earnings**. Because of this they will not require any funds from "Insurance".

Remember, we can retire after 35 years (20 years old + 35 years working = 55 years old at retirement) vs. 67 years under the present Social Security funding plans! We will retire a full ten years earlier than we do now and a full 12 years earlier that the present law allows (for full benefits) in the years when Joe plans to retire!

We actually foresee very few on the disabled list for the full 35 years of potential working time! But those who are or get disabled, should be guaranteed an "average" income much higher than at present! The actual figures can be set by our legislators! The expenses of providing an "average" income (which is far above the allowance presently allocated under Social Security) should easily be covered by the retiree's total pool created by their 10% insurance contributions!

And, note that these are insurance payments to the beneficiary and are therefore treated *by him* as income! The disabled person will be putting 10% of these amounts into *his or her* "POT" and will, therefore, "retire" at age 55 and live off the POT earnings! No one will live off the "insurance" portion of STSS for very long.

LET'S REVIEW!

If all this is making your head swim, let's review briefly: No income taxes, EVER, during your working life! Ten percent of all earnings go into a POT. The POT provides a full salary at retirement for the rest of your life. At your death, the POT is used to pay your life-time taxes! During retirement your POT earnings are "taxed" at 10% (or less if

The End of the Rainbow

figures indicate it can be done) to pay for disabled workers and/or their surviving dependents.

There have been numerous attempts to legislate and\or use in some way the power of savings. All these plans have painted a bright picture of the possibilities embodied in saving. We have added the wonderful twist of using *mandated* savings to entirely replace the Social Security System, with *full* retirement and insurance for disability and premature death AND then use these funds to pay all our personal Income Taxes at our death! In the next chapter we want to explore some of the economic impact of this plan.

This is indeed a powerful way to utilize our capitalism to make for a better way of life for everyone! We can have our cake and eat it, too! It is quite literally A POT OF GOLD--not only for every retired person, but for our nation as a whole. We can have more Federal funds to spend and increase our nation's economic health and growth! **We can all benefit!**

GOVERNMENT

Helping People?

Enslaving People?

Chapter 7 **Rocking Chair Power**

""I had" is a heartache, "I have" a
fountain, You're worth what you saved,
not the million you made."
John B. O'Reilly

Now that you know what the Social Trust Surety System is and have hopefully come to realize that there really can be a POT of gold for everyone, let's explore some of the implications of this revolutionary new approach to government and retirement income.

One of the most obvious and certainly the most socially acceptable effects of STSS is the message and power it gives to the seniors and retirees.

For many years we have been bombarded with the alarming statistics that our aging population would bring our country to financial ruin. The tone of many articles written on the topic comes close to equating our aging population to a "curse"! Our ever increasing retired population is pictured as a "problem" which was going to demand more and more sacrifice from the generations following it so that past promises of retirement income could be met. There were even veiled hints that euthanasia might be acceptable to save our seniors the embarrassment of growing old AND DEPENDENT.

ESTEEMING THE ELDERLY

In many cultures the elderly are held in the highest esteem. In these cultures there is no greater honor than that of being old. Older citizens are treated with the utmost dignity and respect. But for us, even though we love and respect our parents, there is a deep seated prejudice against and a fear of growing old! Aging is seen as a curse, not a blessing!

While the differences between our perceptions of advanced age and those of many others is partly determined by cultural differences, economics does affect our judgements! It is difficult to be respectful and "nice" to a whole group whose very existence and requirements seem to threaten our own well being and economic security!

Under the present Social Security System, the narrowing ratio between the workers (contributors to SS) and the retirees (the recipients of the funds), sets up a climate where the aging of the population is viewed as a time bomb!

The End of the Rainbow

And very frankly it is! Social Security has evolved into a system where the retirees are the "takers" and the workers are the "givers". This makes for the perception that oldsters are financial piranhas, feeding on the younger generation.

Is it any wonder that a climate of virtual hostility exists toward older people? The "system" has produced a whole generation of oldsters who were duped by circumstances into ignoring any real planning for the future. They have been left to depend for their very lives on the ability of the present generation of workers to support them!

CHANGING OUR PERCEPTIONS

Now look at what happens to our perceptions under STSS! Everyone will have a POT of gold on which they can retire at full salary for as long as they live! Suddenly the retirees have become a real ASSET to society, not a perceived liability! They will have enough income to provide their own food, shelter and clothing and even medical insurance. In addition, most will be able to continue purchasing other goods and services, thereby contributing substantial amounts to the GNP! They will be able to afford travel, participate in all kinds of recreational activities, perhaps assist grandchildren with their education as well as availing themselves to their own brand of continuing education, and to a whole host of other economically healthy activities! Those who can do these things now are considered "rich" by society. It will be possible for EVERYONE to be "rich" in the future! The presence of "well off" retirees in our world will stimulate enormous economic opportunities for the entire country. There will be a multitude of new jobs and business enterprises catering to this enormously wealthy group. They will command more wealth and expendable income than any age category has ever had in recorded history!

Because retirees will be almost totally self sufficient, there will be another subtle change in our perceptions of old age. As mom and dad become increasingly unable to care for themselves, they should still be able to have enough income to hire help! Presently, many children are caught between a rock and a hard place when their parents become physically dependent.

On the one hand, parents usually cannot afford any kind of retirement or nursing homes, as these commonly are prohibitively expensive. Government programs (read some form of welfare) or dependence upon children or other family are almost mandatory for mere survival!

The End of the Rainbow

On the other hand, adult children usually cannot AFFORD to take care of parents in their own or their parent's home. As much as most of us love our parents, taking time off to care for them is a financial sacrifice we are unwilling or unable to undertake! Because of this, aging parents are seen as an impending disaster to most children. Not only can parents be a potential emotional drain as life saps their vitality and health, but they can represent a real and tangible economic and financial threat as well!

There will always be sacrifices and emotional hazards which children pay as they consider aging parents. Isn't it grand, therefore, that except in unusual circumstances, they need not be financially burdened as well! If the parents still command a full retirement income, they pose a much lesser threat to the family welfare.

We could see, for example, that a son or daughter, might be "hired" by the parent to take care of them. As an "employee" of the parent, the child would then be allowed to make their 10% contribution to their own POT of the "wages". Even if the parent becomes physically dependent, they could still be making a meaningful contribution to the total family's financial health!

OLD AGE IS AN ASSET NOT A LIABILITY!!

We have outlined this possible scenario to make a point. Financial independence in old age will make a profound change in the way we look at older people! They are and will be as long as they live, assets to their family, community, and world! This change alone will make a big difference on how we view our own aging process! STSS will celebrate the retirees, not fear them!

We, of course, will always be concerned about our health in retirement. But gone will be the fear we now carry of becoming destitute and financially dependent! Just knowing that we have an untouchable POT of gold whose sizable income we can enjoy until we die, gives us a large measure of peace of mind! What a gift to give to ourselves and to all future retirees!

So old age is not a liability to be avoided! Seniors are a great and valuable asset, to be held in high esteem! They will continue to make huge contributions to the overall economy financially.

And, because they are financially liberated, they will be able to contribute time and services to a multitude of worthy community, civic, and religious activities. Volunteerism will become synonymous with the retired! I have known many retirees who dreamed of donating time and services, only to discover that they could not because they were forced to earn supplemental income just to survive!

There is much we could say about the therapeutic value of keeping busy after one retires. What a difference there is, however, between HAVING to work to survive and wanting to work for the contribution one can make! It may make the difference between dreading old age and looking enthusiastically forward to it!

I hope that STSS will see us changing our own attitudes toward retirement. The retirement years should bring us peace and comfort, not dread and foreboding.

The Social Trust Surety System will go a long way toward changing both our own view and the general public's view of aging. Seniors will be esteemed and valued. They will make valuable contributions to our world, both economically and by their very presence as experienced and wise members of our society. They will no longer be feared as possible "takers", but as valuable "givers"!

Retiring?

An adequate income can certainly make a difference in how you live!

Financial independence during retirement can powerfully influence families and society!

Chapter 8 **Free, Free, Debt Free, at Last!**

*"A billion here, a billion there, and pretty
soon you're talking about real money."*
attributed to **Everett M. Dirksen**

The ultimate impact of the Social Trust Surety System
on our Federal budget is almost beyond imagining! The most
immediate result will be the complete removal of Social
Security benefit payments from the budget. In approximately
35 years, 1/3 to 1/2 of the present budget can begin to be
phased out. There will be a few lingering hold-overs from the
old Social Security System. But, every year after that there
will be fewer and fewer of these hold-overs left to collect
benefits.

Also in 35 years, some POT holders will surely die,
leaving the matured POT to be used by the Federal Budget.
Every passing year after that, more and more funds will be
coming in, and fewer and fewer payments will be going out!

There has been a great debate over "entitlements" over
the last few years. So many items in the Federal Budget were
not really negotiable because huge sums were allocated to pay
"promised benefits" to various groups of citizens. The

91

outlook for a balanced budget with "entitlements" hanging over our heads was slim to none! We face, without STSS, a situation where fewer and fewer workers will be required to support more and more "entitled" people! A huge increase in taxes looms if nothing is done and done in a hurry!

EVERYONE WILL BE INDEPENDENTLY WEALTHY!

With the Social Trust Surety System in place this situation is not only solved, but completely turned around! Everyone will have their own POT, a personal trust fund, from which all of their retirement income flows! Each POT holder will have a "golden goose" from which annual earnings flow. Retirement income will not depend on any other tax based support! The retirees will have cut loose the chains which bound the succeeding generation!

With all other factors remaining the same, the National Budget should begin a very noticeable decline in 35 years. Not only will Retirement outlays (presently 49% of the budget) begin to decline, but revenue from maturing POTs will begin to come in. Retirement payments of all kinds, (not just Social Security related ones), and the interest on the

The End of the Rainbow

National Debt account for 63% of the Federal Budget! It will not take long to pay off the National Debt at that rate!

It should be noted that EVERYONE who makes or earns money will have a POT, including all government employees! This makes huge retirement outlays for them, largely unnecessary. It is our contention that ALL "entitlements" should be eliminated. If government salaries and compensation plans do anything, they should include payments to POTS, not some fabulous retirement "parachute" where several years of government service entitle one to huge pensions.

In this way, the government "loans" the money to the employee and will get it back at the employee's death!

ESTIMATING THE FEDERAL BUDGET OF THE FUTURE

Now the question is, can the Personal Income Tax be eliminated? Cutting the Budget by almost 2/3 (it is presently at $1.2 Trillion!) would make the total $444 Billion. This is actually 37% of the present amount, after eliminating entitlements and interest on the National Debt. Will the income from maturing POTs come to $444 Billion?

Let's recall that almost everyone has a POT. Mr. Joe Average on his Spartan salary of $24,000 per year has accumulated approximately $350,000 in his POT! All this, by definition, goes to pay his life-time income tax when he dies. Remember, POT also stands for Prepaid One-time Tax!

In 1992 the death toll in the United States was 2,269,518. Let's assume that this will be approximately the same after POTs have been firmly established. In reality, the increasing population along with an aging population, among whom the mortality rate is actually higher, should push this annual death toll even higher. If 75% of those dying have a POT, there would be a total of 1,600,000 POTs coming into the treasury in any one year. The income total should be well over $5,000,000,000,000 (read Trillion!), a huge surplus! That kind of money could soon add up!

When we look at POT income from another viewpoint, the possibilities are even more dramatic. In almost all cases the amounts being produced by POTs are at least double what the individual would have paid in Personal Income Tax and Social Security payments! Without doing any calculations, collecting twice the amount of money from each "tax payer" would certainly amount to a lot of money. Great things should be able to take place in America when the National Budget takes in double what it previously did and cuts its expenses by more that half! By all calculations, all other forms of "income tax" could be eliminated! When Social Security payments are disregarded, the average person will contribute to their government's coffers over 4 times what they were doing under the "old" system!

A BUDGET SURPLUS?

This projected surplus in the Federal Budget could go a long way toward funding some truly needed projects. We can imagine, for example, a National High Speed Rail system benefitting millions of travelers; Solar and Wind Powered generating stations, capable of supplying cheap, pollution free energy to the entire country; Sea water desalting projects, supplying unlimited water for domestic use and irrigation; Aggressively exploring outer space; funding basic research in science and physics; and funding for research into the causes and cures of the diseases which plague mankind!

The possibilities are endless. We are also in need of constantly updating our infrastructures of roads, highways, bridges, and other public facilities.

It is my sincere hope, that with all these possibilities, we have learned the lessons of the Twentieth Century and NEVER AGAIN BORROW to meet inflated National Budgets! Borrowing and deficit spending are a pit we dare not fall into again!

FINANCING ALL GOVERNMENTS?

There is another possibility with the extra funds generated by the POTs. It is conceivable that all State governments could possibly be financed through POTS funds!

The very thought of life without Income Tax seems alien to us. What would life really be like if we could actually use 90% of our earnings on real goods and services? There is absolutely no doubt in my mind that it would produce an extremely healthy economy. Not only would older people have a life-time income, but earning age families would have more disposable income as well! It truly is a "capitalistic" idea! From our vantage point, the Social Trust Surety System promises a vigorous economy which will benefit everyone.

It also rekindles the hope of an increased Quality of Life for future generations. All previous predictions say our quality of life has been and will continue to decline over the next several generations! STSS promises to reverse this trend!

RESTORING FAITH IN OUR GOVERNMENT

There is another aspect of having POTs. Over the latter part of the Twentieth Century, government was being viewed as more and more intrusive, controlling seemingly every aspect of our lives. The general mood of the voters was one of almost contempt for the "system". While POTs will be mandated, they are certainly a long way from the intrusive way the IRS has invaded our privacy and trampled on so many Civil Rights in an effort to collect taxes! We feel that POTs will go a long way toward restoring confidence in government and renewing respect for our elected officials, who had the profound insight and wisdom to free America financially! POTs will be perceived as "ours" and we will willingly, and even enthusiastically, contribute to them! After all, they are for "my" use and welfare for as long as I live!

What we do *now* can make such a big difference!

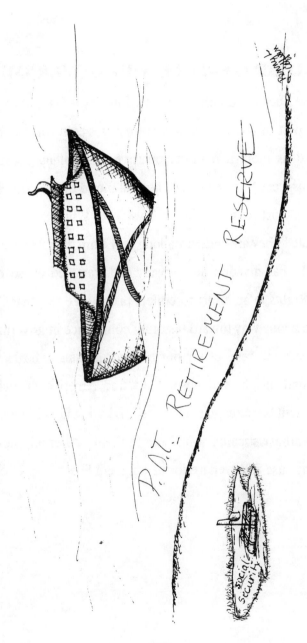

P.O.T. RETIREMENT RESERVE

Social Security

Chapter 9 **Capitol on Capital**

"Common sense is not so common."
Voltaire

I was always taught that our country's economic system was based on capitalism. Capitalism is defined as the ownership, use and control of capital (wealth, money, property, assets, etc.)by private citizens under competitive conditions. We actually talk more about capitalism than we practice it! While we pay lip service to the idea that capitalism is the basis of our free enterprise system, we allow and actually erect barriers and controls to its free functioning in our society. We candidly acknowledge that anyone in our country should be able to accumulate some capital and invest it in ways which will allow it to grow and produce income.

The truth, however, is not really that simple. Much of our productive activity is based on economic factors not related to use of capital in a pure supply and demand atmosphere. While free enterprise, with supply and demand pressures, certainly influences all of us, a much more subtle "law" is at work. It is called *Taxes*! Our form of capitalism is channelled, influenced and shaped by the taxes society has decreed! Taxes, quite simply, alter the playing field on which capitalism is practiced!

DECISIONS BASED ON TAXES

Many American family and business decisions are based on tax considerations! Typically we have one eye on the tax laws when we plan things. We are anxious to minimize or eliminate the tax consequences of our activities. Even the decision to get married or to have children often entails a look at how our taxes will be effected! Of course, many of us get married and have children anyway, but we *do* take taxes into consideration! Business often decides on its courses of action on the basis of what is "deductible" or "allowed" on their tax return! Tax attorneys are kept busy helping both individuals and businesses plan strategies to keep tax laws from eroding income unnecessarily.

Not only do we plan many activities around the tax laws, tax dollars have a huge impact on our economy in the way they are spent! Many great industries and businesses have emerged, thrived or died as a result of the spending policies of a taxing body, the chief being the U.S. Government.

Huge industries were impacted by our nation's entrance into Space exploration, for example! Since billions of dollars were directed to the space effort, companies were created or restructured to take advantage of the newly available money! Even a casual observer could conclude that tax money influenced where many business enterprises concentrated their efforts!

We should point out that there is very little that our proposed Social Trust Surety System will do to influence the way tax money is *spent*. Government bodies get their funds from many different sources, but the projects they endorse, support and underwrite will skew economic development and growth, just as surely as fertilizer thrown on the lawn will affect the pattern of growth of the grass!

MORE DISPOSABLE INCOME TO SPEND!

It should be no surprise to point out that the general public, under STSS, will have a great deal more money to spend than ever before! Instead of having at least 25% of wages going to taxes (which is the typical "bite" under our present system) and still having to provide for retirement, Mr. Joe Average will have only 10% demanded of him and THAT is going toward his retirement! Each wage earner will have an average of 15% more money to spend! This huge increase in expendable income will influence our economy in dramatic ways! In the past, even small cuts in the tax rates had a very powerful positive economic impact.

The Social Trust Surety System will, however, have a profoundly negative effect on the government's ability to shape public and social policy through its tax laws! Gone will be the ability to exempt certain forms of income from taxes, or to treat certain expenditures as deductions. In short, those who envision government as the great manager of all things, will be grossly disappointed in STSS!

Let's look, for example, at the government's role in manipulating credit. In the days when economic growth was viewed as the ultimate good, borrowing to stimulate purchases was avidly encouraged. Government did this by making all interest deductible at income tax time! Buying things on credit was easy and economically desirable to Mr. Joe Average because the interest he paid was a deductible item when he figured his taxes.

The country benefited because this stimulated a wave of spending on goods and services. The increased demand boosted the economy as factories and business geared up to meet the increased purchasing power of the consumer! It worked! As a matter of fact, it often worked too well. The amount of consumer debt sky rocketed and threatened the very economy it was supposed to stimulate! Savings were ignored. After all, savings earned interest and interest WAS taxed! Borrowing and credit entailed paying interest, and interest was deductible! (This is just another illustration of how our actions are influenced by tax laws!)

When the consumer debt was perceived as a threat to the economy, lawmakers removed the provision that interest payments were deductible expenses!

An interesting side note is that mortgage interest is still deductible under most circumstances. The reason? Home ownership is considered a healthy and desirable public policy! Tax laws do have had a powerful impact on the economic actions of American tax payers!

A LOOK AT OUR POLITICIANS

Let's make this observation in passing. Lawmakers have apparently taken little stock in encouraging savings in the American public. In the first place, interest on earnings has traditionally been fully taxed! Except for a brief experiment with IRAs, where there are no tax consequences on the interest until the funds are withdrawn, there has been no serious attempt made to encourage savings through the tax laws!

I tend to be rather cynical about elected officials anyway! While most public servants are truly dedicated and honestly trying to achieve a better world, there are those who, it seems to me, cannot think beyond the next election. To these short sighted politicians, it makes much more sense to either create a problem or ignore one, if it makes them "look good" in the public's eye at the next election. In other words, collect taxes now, whether it is in the long range interest of the country or not. If that happens to create even worse problems down the road, that only gives them a chance to be "heroes" and come up with more band-aid solutions THEN! Long range thinking and planning are for those who have no stakes in the next election! I hope we will soon see a whole new generation of true statesmen and remove from our vocabulary the word "politician" and the self serving image that congers up for us! Perhaps adapting STSS would go a long way toward restoring my faith in our legislaturers!

GETTING AWAY FROM THE SOCIALISTIC SNARES

The philosophy of dealing only with "now" problems without regard for long range consequence has dealt the capital gains tax a devastating blow! Without the investment of capital our economic system would break down entirely! The capital gains tax was an attempt to take this simple truth into account. Investment was encouraged by limiting the amount of taxes which could be imposed on them. Whether intended or not, removing the incentives of capital gains has subtly changed the capitalist emphasis of our economy! This, coupled with other less subtle changes, tends to shape us into a more socialistic economy. From analyzing my own feelings and the actions of my peers, I can truthfully say, there is very little incentive to save and invest! Those who DO invest face additional obstacles and frustrations. It is surprising to me that any NEW venture which requires capital can even get off the ground! Maybe lawmakers should investigate WHY most new business fail---and then pass laws which ENCOURAGE investment rather than DISCOURAGE it!

The point is, there is very little doubt that tax laws do and will continue to influence the economic behavior of all citizens! We make very few personal financial decisions of any consequence without considering the effects of taxes on that decision! Multiply that personal decision by millions of tax payers who are also making similar decisions and you have a powerful economic influence!

A MARKET DRIVEN ECONOMY??

Now imagine an economy where personal income taxes, whether imposed, delayed or abated, play no part in economic decision making! Because we have grown up in an era where taxes have ALWAYS been a factor, it is difficult for us to visualize such a scenario. Yet, we have to think through the consequences of the lawmakers' inability to influence public policy through the imposition of taxes! Is this what we want?

Realistically, we must admit that a "hands off" policy in this area could have both positive and negative effects. For example, would we, as Americans, still invest in homes if the interest from the mortgages necessary to purchase them were not tax deductible? Would we still give to charitable and religious organizations if there were no tax rewards for so doing, especially for the larger donations? What would be the effect on the lobbying efforts of special interest groups, much of which is directed toward special consideration of tax matters? Would it affect the way we view medical and dental expenses? What changes in attitude would we have in America toward many other taxes if they no longer influenced our personal income taxes?

It is these very questions and the UNKNOWN ANSWERS which create fear of change in lawmakers and in us ordinary citizens as well! It is this fear of the unknown which has dampened our discussion of replacing the personal income tax with a flat rate tax or a national sales tax! In either of these possible replacements for the income tax, very little "fine tuning", "manipulation", or "downright meddling" (choose the right wording depending on your political philosophy!) would be possible on the collection side of federal taxes.

My own guess is that given a truly "free market" without the "guidance" of tax laws, public policy issues would either disappear or could be addressed in entirely new and creative ways! Using tax laws to manipulate public policy has created many different situations, both favorable and unfavorable. I am certain that our legislatures can come up with creative ways outside the tax laws to achieve the same ends.

The issue of home ownership is an example. It is my guess that the pride of ownership would far outweigh any tax incentives the government could ever offer! There are some very important economic advantages of ownership, including the building of equity and long range security because of that equity. There are also those for whom renting would now make more sense. Frequent moves, for example, where buying and selling a home often imposes a severe hardship, would tend to direct a family or person toward some non-ownership alternative. In any case, decisions about owning or renting would be made by personal preference and circumstances, not on some public policy shaped by taxation!

We would also find it difficult to imagine a world where business decisions would be made without the lengthy and cumbersome analysis of how taxes would be impacted by those decisions! It seems to me that some of the grossly inequitable situations between "for profit" and "not-for-profit" organizations would be eliminated and a whole new level playing field could be established where value and costs would be the only considerations, not who paid or did not pay taxes! I feel this would open up a whole new area and era of investment opportunities uncomplicated by tax laws!

This freedom from taxation, at least from income taxes, would give us a truly market driven economy. Our economics would not be distorted and shaped by tax laws, but by supply and demand. There is no doubt that it would affect investments, savings, giving, buying, selling, owning, renting, and even health care decisions. But these decisions would be based on hard economic merit, not tax policies!

GETTING GOVERNMENT OFF OUR BACKS

This whole issue boils down to one which has recently dominated much of our political debates: government's intrusion into our personal lives! Many have voiced frustration with "Big Government" poking into every aspect of their lives. This is especially true in the areas where the IRS has assumed an almost untouchable government role, completely isolated from the rules and laws which govern everyone else! The IRS has unbelievable powers to seize property, assets, and records, without regard to the proprieties other law enforcement agencies must follow!

Adaption of the Social Trust Surety System with its consequent removal of the IRS would certainly go a long way toward restoring some confidence and credibility to our Federal Government.

Someone made the passing remark that our Congress would never even think of doing anything to remove the IRS from our lives! Doing so would remove our most hated symbol of government and open the Congress up to being NEXT on the list! Maybe so, but removing itself from annual discussions on how to impose more taxes on the citizens and how to manipulate public policy through taxation would go a long way toward restoring public confidence in our Congress!

The problem is not so much government institutions as such, it's their systematic destruction of our human and civil rights we object to! Once Congress can begin to operate and deal with surpluses in government funds instead of deficits, perhaps its image can be reborn in the American taxpayer's mind!

Government has indeed been a fertilizer on our economic lawn! Government has profoundly influenced many, if not most, of our economic decisions. It has been responsible for vigorous growth in some areas, for economic death in others. All of us have learned that fertilizer can both help and harm. For some of us, who grew up on the farm, fertilizer can often be identified by a whole other name! By getting out of the business of taxing personal income, perhaps Congress can restore the "good" name of Government fertilizer!

We should also add that paying taxes on our earnings and profits would be a viewed in an entirely different light! POT contributions would be seen as a highly desirable activity! Taxes (in our case the 10% paid into OUR own POT) would no longer be perceived as a drain on our income and a deterrent to our own well being! Payments would be deemed as a wise and prudent investment in our own future. The natural incentive would be to add to our own POT, not avoid or evade doing so! It just seems reasonable that this approach would be a major step toward restoring honesty and integrity in our society. Of course, that is a whole different issue---or is it?

**Both plans will get you there.
Which one is the best choice?**

The Present
Balancing Act To
Retirement

The Solid Plan
To Retirement

Chapter 10 **Capitalizing on Capital**

"The republic is a dream.
Nothing happens unless first a dream."
Carl Sandburg

As you have discovered, the Social Trust Surety System has a profoundly positive effect on the personal economic life of every worker in America. The impact on the business world is almost as dramatic! The implementation of the Social Trust Surety System will directly influence the economy of the entire world!

This process begins because everyone who has ever had an income will have a POT. The amount of accumulated capital that those POTs represent is staggering, to put it mildly. It means that each and every average American will have nearly $1 million to be invested! This is an incredible amount of wealth! This wealth can, in turn, be used to start up and expand business both at home and abroad!

Many new and innovative ideas are never developed because capital is not available. New business ventures are

113

usually labeled "high risk" and investors are reluctant to gamble when the odds of success are so remote. The figures show, however, that *under capitalization* is the greatest cause of new business failures! By having more capital available in the first place, fewer new businesses would fail! The result should be an explosion of new American businesses. The resulting technological and industrial edge this abundance of capital would give us would help us regain our world leadership!

The lack of adequate capital has been a huge detriment to our economy for some time. We simply lack the large pool of savings necessary for robust growth. As a result, the money for investments has increasingly come from outside our own country! Our lack of investment money has encouraged foreign interests to invest in the United States. Oil rich nations who were looking for places to put their funds, found a ready market for their wealth. Oil money bought up vast amounts of property, land and businesses over the last several decades. The same thing is true of Japanese capital. We have seen foreign investments thrive and flourish in the United States. Much of this because we ourselves lack the savings and capital to compete with these "outside" sources!

Of course, investing from any and all sources has

produced jobs for our labor force. Investments make business possible and businesses have produced jobs and jobs stimulate our economy. These businesses also produced goods and services which we have benefited from. Most of us understand that in order to have jobs and economic development, there must be some capital investment! The bad news is that we are not always able to supply enough of that capital from our own resources. This means that the EARNINGS from those investments, more than likely, did not stay in the USA! Now instead of stimulating the economy, the profits are increasingly leaving our country! Now we can begin to see the negative effects of not having vast savings of our own!

An essentially limitless supply of capital would begin an continuous round of business expansion with its accompanying offer of new jobs and new products to benefit all of us! There is no doubt that huge amounts of available investment money would create a robust and healthy national economy.

EXPORTING CAPITAL

The implications are that then we would have surplus funds to invest. We can visualize how domestic growth would take place, and then we would be able to export capital to the rest of the world!

When American capital is able to invest in foreign economic development, both countries would benefit! Not only could poor countries rely on American interests to develop and encourage their local economies, but American investors would benefit by seeing a healthy world economy and a good investment return!

Properly approached, POTs could have a decided impact on world economic development. If it is really true that economics, unemployment, starvation, and quality of life issues have started wars, the alleviation of these should certainly help the cause of peace! The human race will undoubtedly always find something to fight over, but when wealth is properly shared and used, some of our present conflicts will become moot! There are those who feel strongly that the proper distribution of wealth is the key to justice and peace in the world. Certainly the Social Trust Surety System is not a cure all, but the long term prospect of an amply supply of investment capital would go a long way toward achieving economic justice. Not only will the immense economic power of POTs influence world economics and peace, but there should also be a very broad and positive impact on our own quality of life!

DEVELOPING NEW TECHNOLOGY

The United States has been one of the world leaders in developing new technology. Having the necessary capital for serious research and development should secure for us the undisputed role of technological pioneer! When our scientific community and our industry leaders keep their leading edge of discovery alive, the United States will continue to be a world class leader in new technology!

To some extent, our "edge" has suffered recently. We have lost a great deal of momentum in the electronics industry, for example, to Japan. This was simply because we lacked adequate capital to invest in intensive research and development. The initiative was lost and the electronics industry shifted to those who had done their homework and invested their money in research and development!!

We could point out other fields where we have lost our economic advantage and superiority, largely because we lacked the necessary funds for research and development. Whenever any industry becomes content to do things the same

117

old way, it begins to lose out; There are not too many buggy whip manufacturers left!

The same thing could be said for basic scientific research. The super-collider is a recent case in point. The project was "killed" because it was to be funded entirely with government funds and there simply were not enough of these funds to go around! Would the project have gone on had there been businesses interested in cooperating by contributing research and development funds? Your guess is as good as mine, but I choose to think that adequate capital (savings) would have rescued the project!

Many other examples of basic research projects which go begging could be cited. There simply are not enough funds around to finance all the projects necessary to discover all the things about the world we live in! It is only when adequate funding and total freedom to explore is given to such research that truly breathtaking discoveries can made! Research cannot be undertaken without plenty of capital --and plenty of capital cannot exist without savings --and POTs represent savings!

The use of capital could also dramatically influence our health. One of the chronic victims of scarce funds is research into the causes and cures of the many afflictions of mankind! There simply are not enough private funds around today to finance all the Research and Development necessary to push some of these scourges aside forever!

We need research into genetics, cancer, AIDS, diabetes, heart and cardio-vascular diseases, aging, arthritis, and a host of other ailments and afflictions! All of us could benefit greatly from the capital generated by the Social Trust Surety System!

Capital is at the very heart of our economic life. Without it, business and industry would shrivel up and die. Capital is needed to inject new ideas and discoveries into the marketplace. We all benefit when the economy is healthy. We all benefit when we are physically able to ward off debilitating illness and ailments! We need capital to keep alive the American dream.

With so many benefits which the Social Trust Surety System promises to bring us, can't we just get it started? Why don't we just begin now and start reaping the rewards of saving for our future?

Unfortunately, the answer is not all that simple! We need to explore, "How do we get from here to there?" We will begin that process in the next section of our book.

Capital

Properly used and nurtured
can bring us all prosperity!

SECTION III

GETING FROM

HERE

TO THERE

Chapter 11 **The Possible Dream!**

"No one can be perfectly free till all are free;
No one can be perfectly moral till all are moral;
No one can be perfectly happy till all are happy."
Herbert Spencer

There were times when "getting there" seemed to be almost impossible. It is rather easy for us to visualize the Social Trust Surety System as it should be after it is up and running for several years. As a matter of fact, the whole system is uncomplicated and involves a minimum of red tape and government regulation. Because of the enormous benefits to every worker, enforcing the 10% contribution would not be onerous or difficult. If we could start the Social Trust Surety System today and "piggy-back" it on top of everything else we are doing right now, there would be no problems.

In reality, this approach to getting the Social Trust Surety System started is not all that bad an idea! It would involve committing another 10% of our incomes to a mandated government program. To balance this, we must realize that our present Social Security Administration will be losing money from 2012 on, and will be completely out of funds by 2030! Even if we did NOTHING, more of our earnings and wages would have to be committed to the Federal Budget just to save Social Security! So, whether we choose to save Social Security or replace it with something far better, the bottom line is, it will cost us more in the next few years. The choice is, do we get something for our money, or do we opt for more of the same?

REJECT SOCIAL SECURITY FUNDING INCREASES

By allowing Social Security to die a natural death by refusing increased funding for it, we could easily begin our STSS program. Mr. Joe Average and his employer might, in the early years, cooperate to come up with the required 10% contribution to Joe's POT. This may well be within or less than the amounts Social Security would require to keep it solvent! It is a given, however, that Joe and his employer will be required to pay more in the future whether or not STSS is adopted. It should be an easy choice, because with the Social

The End of the Rainbow

Trust Surety System, we are getting a huge return for our extra money!

CREATIVE SOCIAL SECURITY COVERAGE

We can also hasten the "retirement age" by allowing the first few years of maturing POTs to be paid out as annuities. ADDITIONAL years may be subtracted from the "contribution years" by setting the annuities to the same level of payments allowed by Social Security. Using these guidelines, we could begin the change-over for *everyone* under age 40 and expect retirement age to be 67 as anticipated under the present Social Security laws. Those 40 and over would continue to be covered by the present Social Security System. When they reach full retirement age of 67, they would be eligible for the benefits accorded them by Social Security. Those in this category of Social Security coverage would also be required to have POTs.

At their death, the POTs could be paid into the Social Security Trust Fund to help pay benefits for all those still receiving benefits. By doing this, very little or no changes would be required to keep Social Security solvent until all those who are eligible to receive benefits are gone!

Should there be any deficits, and remember these are already scheduled to occur between 2013 and 2030, they could be covered by a Federal Budget appropriation or "borrowing" by the Social Security System. The beautiful part of such a plan is that POTs will continue to grow for this age group because there are no withdrawals of earnings. The longer one in this age group lives, and the longer they are receiving Social Security benefits, the more their POTs will contribute to the Social Security System!

By the time the last survivor of Social Security benefits dies, there should be a large surplus of funds from these "maturing" POTs. These surplus funds can be used to pay back any "borrowed funds" to the Federal Treasury and become the beginning of the reduction of the National Debt!

ENACT THE LEGISLATION

So the very first step in making POTs our retirement vehicle and our replacement for the personal Income Tax is to pass legislation requiring everyone to establish a POT. This would be in lieu of tampering in any way with Social Security contributions or benefits! Everyone earning any kind of income would be required to have a POT and contribute 10% of that income to their POT.

126

CONTROL EARLY RETIREMENT IN THE BEGINNING

Now we have another problem. After 35 years of contributing to their POT, most workers will want to retire! This means that in the 36th year after establishing POTs as our "way of life" there will be workers of all ages who have contributed for 35 years and are eligible to retire at full salary! Let's say that this program kicks off in the year 2000. If someone had stated at age 18 in the year 2000 and worked for 35 years, they would want to retire at age 53 in 2035. The problem for the national economy is that everyone over that age would also want to retire in 2035. If you were 32 in 2000, you would retire in 2035 at age 67. So everyone between the ages of 18 and 32 in the year 2000 would want to retire in 2035! The blow to our work force would undoubtedly be devastating. By setting a minimum age for retirement and reducing it every year, such a scenario would be avoided. Thus in 2035 you would have to be at least 65 to retire with full benefits; in 2036, 63; in 2036, 61; in 2037, 59; in 2038, 57 and in 2039, 55. This slight delay in utilizing one's POT would actually benefit the worker. For example, if someone worked an estimated 10 years longer, or for 45 years, they would actually double their POT retirement earnings!   In any case, the requirements for retirement would be less than under the present Social Security Administration laws! Only in the very first year that POTs mature, would workers be required to wait until they are 67 to begin their retirement at full benefits. We feel, given the added incentives of working over the 35 year MINIMUM, many workers will opt to work longer. Another 5 years of contributing to the POT will increase the average worker's annual retirement earnings an additional 50%! Now the prospect at retirement is not only to receive a FULL SALARY BENEFIT, but some additional years over the required 35 years, means retiring at MORE THAN FULL SALARY! This "overtime" not only adds substantially to the worker's retirement income, but also increases the value of the POT which goes to pay their life-time taxes at death! Both the individual worker and the government win!

Would you believe that there have been attempts by Congress to allow individuals to "divert" Social Security funds into private investments! While most of these efforts to "reform" Social Security have fallen on deaf ears, there have been those who realized that the American worker was being essentially short changed. While it is not within the scope of this book to analyze these past attempts, we can point out that

The End of the Rainbow

our approach is not entirely new. We have simply gone beyond the vague feeling of dissatisfaction with the way things are, and proposed a perfectly logical and painless way of "having our cake and eating it, too"!

SOME SACRIFICE IS INVOLVED

Granted, there will be a whole generation which will have to live under two different "systems". Yet, their "load" will not be appreciably more than it would have been had Social Security been "rescued"! The rewards, however, are enormously more attractive with the Social Trust Surety System in place!

Note that the promise of no personal income tax cannot be given to the first POT users. Government will have to be supported until POTs begin to mature. There simply is no other way, UNLESS some of the ideas relating to a National Sales Tax take hold. In reality, a National Sales Tax would begin the transition process much more smoothly, as it could be phased out gradually as POTs begin to go into the national coffers!

CLAIM YOUR P O T

So, what do you think? Is there a POT of gold at the end of your rainbow? Not if you merely THINK it is a good idea! It is time for us to let all of our elected officials on the national level know what we want!

This book was meant not only to stimulate your thinking, but to goad you into action! Unless we start a Social Trust Surety System NOW, we stand to lose our American Way of Life! If you believe we can do better, ACT! Write, phone, visit your Senators and Representatives. Work on a local level to elect those who share your vision for a POT of gold for everyone!

Perhaps our generation can leave a real legacy to our children! The prospects of a brighter tomorrow is certainly better by far than a world filled with almost insurmountable debt. Even our own debts are often difficult to handle, let alone debts which our parents have piled up! The Social Trust Surety System does indeed promise a pot of gold for everyone. But like all promises, someone has to take the steps to execute the plan, or the dreams will vanish like a rainbow!

Chapter 12 **Getting Congressional Action**

The people who have reviewed my book and commented on its content have nearly all told me the same thing. It is an excellent concept, but it leaves no room for people in government to get their hands on the money! They think that the chances of passage into law are, therefore, very slim!

While I am often discouraged about what political action can actually acheive, I think that passage of the Social Trust Surety System is not a hopeless case! If enough citizens insist that their congressional leaders act on the proposals we have outlined, we can be assured that even slow moving and often very short-sighted political machinery will be set into motion!

It is extremely important, therefore, that you express to YOUR elected leaders the importance of looking 35 years to the future and overhauling our retirement programs NOW. We may not all be around for the great benefits, but we can be certain that our children and grand children will be! Write these legislators, send them a copy of the book, call them, attend meetings where they are speaking and express your convictions until SOMETHING is done!

The following list of senators and representatives from each state was current as of April, 1997. There may have been some changes and we appologize in advance for any errors, ommissions and changes which we were not able to incorporate into this listing!

THE SENATE

ALABAMA
Jeff Sessions
Dirksen Senate
OfficeBldg. #B34
Washington, DC 20510
FAX 202-224-3149

Richard C. Shelby
Hart Senate Office Bldg.
#110
Washington, DC 20510
FAX 202-224-3416

ALASKA
Ted Stevens
Hart Senate Office Bldg.
#522
Washington, DC 20510
FAX 202-224-2354

Frank H. Murkowski
Hart Senate Office Bldg.
#706
Washington, DC 20510
FAX 202-224-5301

ARIZONA
John McCain
Russell Senate Office
Bld. #241
Washington, DC 20510
FAX 202-228-2862

Jon Kyl
Hart Senate Office Bldg.
#702
Washington, DC 20510
FAX 202-228-1239

ARKANSAS
Dale Bumpers
Dirksen Senate Office
Bld #229
Washington, DC 20510
FAX 202-224-6435

Tim Hutchison
Hart Senate Office Bld
#708
Washington, DC 20510

CALIFORNIA
Dianne Feinstein
Hart Senate Office Bldg
#331
Washington, DC 20510
FAX 202-228-3954

Barbara Boxer
Hart Senate Office Bldg
#112
Washington, DC 20510
FAX 202-228-3789

COLORADO
Wayne Allard
Hart Senate Office Bldg
716
Washington, DC 20510
FAX 202-224-6471

Ben Nighthorse Campbell
Russell Senate Office Bld
380
Washington, DC 20510
FAX 202-224-1933

CONNECTICUT
Christopher J. Dodd
Russell Senate Office Bld
#444
Washington, DC 20510
FAX 202-224-1083

Joseph I. Lieberman
Hart Senate Office Bld
#316
Washington, DC 20510
FAX 202-224-9750

DELAWARE
William V. Roth, Jr.
Hart Senate Office Bldg
#104
Washington, DC 20510
FAX 202-228-0354

Joseph R. Biden, Jr.
Russel Senate Office Bld
#221
Washington, DC 20510
FAX 202-224-0139

FLORIDA
Bob Graham
Hart Senate Office Bldg
#524
Washington, DC 20510
FAX 202-224-2237

Connie Mack
Hart Senate Office Bldg
517
Washington, DC 20510
FAX 202-224-8022

The End of the Rainbow

GEORGIA
Max Cleland
Dirksen Senate Office
Bld #463
Washington, DC 20510
FAX 202-224-0072

Paul Coverdell
Russell Senate Office
Bldg # 200
Washington, DC 20510
FAX 202-228-3783

HAWAII
Daniel K. Inouye
Hart Senate Office Bldg
722
Washington, DC 20510
FAX 202-224-6747

Daniel K. Akaka
Hart Senate Office Bldg
720
Washington, DC 20510
FAX 202-224-2126

IDAHO
Larry E. Craig
Hart Senate Office Bldg
313
Washington, DC 20510
FAX 202-228-1067

Dirk Kempthorne
Dirksen Senate Office
Bld #367
Washington, DC 20510
FAX 202-224-5893

ILLINOIS
Richard Durbin
Russell Senate Office Bld
#267
Washington, DC 20510

Carol Moseley-Braun
Hart Senate Office Bldg
#320
Washington, DC 20510
FAX 202-224-2626

INDIANA
Richard G. Lugar
Hart Senate Office Bldg
#306
Washington, DC 20510
FAX 202-224-0630

Daniel R. Coats
Russell Senate Office Bld
#404
Washington, DC 20510
FAX 202-224-4137

IOWA
Charles E. Grassley
Hart Senate Office Bldg
#135
Washington, DC 20510
FAX 202-224-6020

Tom Harkin
Hart Senate Office Bldg
#531
Washington, DC 20510
FAX 202-224-9369

KANSAS
San Brownback
Hart Senate Office Bldg
#141
Washington, DC 20510
FAX 202-228-1265

Pat Roberts
Dirksen Senate Office
Bld #116
Washington, DC 20510
FAX 202-224-3514

KENTUCKY
Wendell H. Ford
Russell Senate Office Bld
#173A
Washington, DC 20510
FAX 202-224-0046

Mitch McConnell
Russell Senate Office Bld
#361A
Washington, DC 20510
FAX 202-224-2499

LOUISIANA
Mary L. Landrieu
Hart Senate Office Bldg
#825
Washington, DC 20510
FAX 202-224-9735

John B. Breaux
Hart Senate Office Bldg
#516
Washington, DC 20510
FAX 202-228-2577

MAINE
Susan Collins
Dirksen Senate Office
Bld B40 #4
Washington, DC 20510
FAX 202-224-2693

Olympia J. Snowe
Russell Senate Office Bld
#495
Washington, DC 20510
FAX 202-224-1946

MARYLAND
Paul S. Sarbanes
Hart Senate Office Bld
#309
Washington, DC 20510
FAX 202-224-1651

Barbara A. Mikulski
Hart Senate Office Bld
#709
Washington, DC 20510
FAX 202-224-8858

MASSACHUSETTS
Edward M. Kennedy
Russell Senate Office Bld
#315
Washington, DC 20510
FAX 202-224-2417

John Kerry
Russell Senate Office Bld
#421
Washington, DC 20510
FAX 202-224-8525

Getting Congressional Action

MICHIGAN
Carl Levin
Russell Senate Office Bld
#459
Washington, DC 20510
FAX 202-224-1388

Spencer Abraham
Dirksen Senate Office
Bld #245
Washington, DC 20510
FAX 202-224-8834

MINNESOTA
Paul Wellstone
Hart Senate Office Bld
#717
Washington, DC 20510
FAX 202-224-8438

Rod Grams
Dirksen Senate Office
Bld #261
Washington, DC 20510
FAX 202-228-0956

MISSISSIPPI
Thad Cochran
Russell Senate Office Bld
#326
Washington, DC 20510
FAX 202-224-9450

Trent Lott
Russell Senate Office Bld
#487
Washington, DC 20510
FAX 202-224-2262

MISSOURI
Christopher S. Bond
Russell Senate Office Bld
#293
Washington, DC 20510
FAX 202-224-8149

John Ashcroft
Russell Senate Office Bld
#170
Washington, DC 20510
FAX 202-228-5126

MONTANA
Max Baucus
Hart Senate Office Bld
#511
Washington, DC 20510
FAX 202-224-1974

Conrad Burns
Dirksen Senate Office
Bld #187
Washington, DC 20510
FAX 202-224-8594

NEBRASKA
Chuck Hagel
Dirksen Senate Office
Bld B40 #3
Washington, DC 20510
FAX 202-224-5213

J. Robert Kerrey
Hart Senate Office Bld
#303
Washington, DC 20510
FAX 202-224-7645

NEVADA
Harry Reid
Hart Senate Office Bld
#324
Washington, DC 20510
FAX 202-224-7327

Richard H. Bryan
Russell Senate Office Bld
#364
Washington, DC 20510
FAX 202-224-1867

NEW HAMPSHIRE
Robert C., Smith
Dirksen Senate Office
Bld #332
Washington, DC 20510
FAX 202-224-1353

Judd Gregg
Russell Senate Office Bld
#393
Washington, DC 20510
FAX 202-224-4952

NEW JERSEY
Robert G. Torricelli
Hart Senate Office Bld
#728
Washington, DC 20510
FAX 202-224-8567

Frank R. Lautenberg
Hart Senate Office Bld
#506
Washington, DC 20510
FAX 202-224-9707

NEW MEXICO
Pete V. Domenici
Hart Senate Office Bld
#328
Washington, DC 20510
FAX 202-224-7371

Jeff Bingaman
Hart Senate Office Bld
#703
Washington, DC 20510
FAX 202-224-2852

NEW YORK
Daniel Patrick Moynihan
Russell Senate Office Bld
#464
Washington, DC 20510
FAX 202-228-0406

Alfonse M. D'Amato
Hart Senate Office Bld
#520
Washington, DC 20510
FAX 202-224-5871

NORTH CAROLINA
Jesse Helms
Dirksen Senate Office
Bld #403
Washinton, DC 20510
FAX 202-228-1339

Lauch Faircloth
Hart Senate Office Bldg
#317
Washington, DC 20510
FAX 202-224-7406

134

The End of the Rainbow

NORTH DAKOTA
Kent Conrad
Hart Senate Office Bld
#724
Washington, DC 20510
FAX 202-224-7776

Byron L. Dorgan
Hart Senate Office Bld
#713
Washington, DC 20510
FAX 202-224-1193

OHIO
John Glenn
Hart Senate Office Bld
#503
Washington, DC 20510
FAX 202-224-7983

Mike DeWine
Russell Senate Office Bld
#140
Washington, DC 20510
FAX 202-224-6519

OKLAHOMA
Don Nickles
Hart Senate Office Bld
#133
Washington, DC 20510
FAX 202-224-6008

James M. Imhofe
Russell Senate Office Bld
#453
Washington, DC 20510
FAX 202-228-0380

OREGON
Gordon Smith
Dirksen Senate Office
Bld B40 #2
Washington, DC 20510
FAX 202-228-3997

Ron Wyden
Russell Senate Office Bld
#259
Washington, DC 20510
FAX 202-228-2717

PENNSYLVANIA
Arlen Specter
Hart Senate Office Bld
#530
Washington, DC 20510
FAX 202-228-4516

Rick Santorum
Russell Senate Office Bld
120
Washington, DC 20510
FAX 202-228-0604

RHODE ISLAND
Jack Reed
Russell Senate Office Bld
#339
Washington, DC 20510
FAX 202-224-4680

John H. Chafee
Dirksen Senate Office
Bld #505
Washington, DC 20510
FAX 202-228-3976

SOUTH CAROLINA
Strom Thurmond
Russell Senate Office Bld
#217
Washington, DC 20510
FAX 202-224-1300

Ernest F. Hollings
Russell Senate Office Bld
#125
Washington, DC 20510
FAX 202-224-4293

SOUTH DAKOTA
Tim Johnson
Hart Senate Office Bld
#528
Washington, DC 20510
FAX 202-228-0368

Tom Daschle
Hart Senate Office Bld
#510
Washington, DC 20510
FAX 202-224-2047

TENNESSEE
Fred Thompson
Dirksen Senate Office
Bld #523
Washington, DC 20510
FAX 202-228-3679

Bill Frist
Dirksen Senate Office
Bld #565
Washington, DC 20510
FAX 202-228-1264

TEXAS
Phil Gramm
Russell Senate Office Bld
#370
Washington, DC 20510
FAX 202-228-2856

Kay Bailey Hutchison
Russell Senate Office Bld
#283
Washington, DC 20510
FAX 202-224-0776

UTAH
Orrin G. Hatch
Russell Senate Office Bld
#131
Washington, DC 20510
FAX 202-224-6331

Robert F. Bennett
Dirksen Senate Office
Bld #431
Washington, DC 20510
FAX 202-224-4908

VERMONT
Patrick J. Leahy
Russell Senate Office Bld
#433
Washington, DC 20510
FAX 202-224-3595

James M. Jeffords
Hart Senate Office Bld
#513
Washington, DC 20510
FAX 202-228-0338

135

VIRGINIA
John W. Warner
Russell Senate Office Bld
#225
Washington, DC 20510
FAX 202-224-6295

Charles S. Robb
Russell Senate Office Bld
#154
Washington, DC 20510
FAX 202-224-8689

WASHINGTON
Slate Gorton
Hart Senate Office Bld
#730
Washington, DC 20510
FAX 202-224-9393

Patty Murray
Russell Senate Office Bld
#111
Washington, DC 20510
FAX 202-224-0238

WEST VIRGINIA
Robert C. Byrd
Hart Senate Office Bld
#311
Washington, DC 20510
FAX 202-224-8070

John D. Rockerfeller IV
Hart Senate Office Bld
#109
Washington, DC 20510
FAX 202-224-7665

WISCONSIN
Herb Kohl
Hart Senate Office Bld
#330
Washington, DC 20510
FAX 202-224-9787

Russell D. Feingold
Hart Senate Office Bld
#502
Washington, DC 20510
FAX 202-224-2725

WYOMING
Mike Enzi
Hart Senate Office Bld
#116
Washington, DC 20510

Craig Thomas
Hart Senate Office Bld
#302
Washington, DC 20510
FAX 202-224-1724

THE HOUSE

CHOB= Cannon House Office Building, #   , Washington, DC 20515
LHOB=Longworth House Office Building, # , Washington, DC 20515
RHOB=Rayburn House Office Building, #   , Washington, DC 20515

ALABAMA
1. Sonny Callahan
   RHOB -2418
   FAX 202-225-0562
2. Terry Everett
   CHOB -208
   FAX 202-225-2901
3. Bob Riley
   CHOB -510
   FAX 202-225-5827
4. Robert Aderholt
   LHOB -1007
   FAX 202-225-5587
5. Robert E. Cramer, Jr
   CHOB -236
   FAX 202-225-4392
6. Spencer Bachus
   CHOB -127
   FAX 202-225-2082
7. Earl F. Hilliard
   LHOB -1007
   FAX 202-226-0772

ALASKA
   Don Young
   RHOB -2331
   FAX 202-225-0542

ARIZONA
1. Matt Salmon
   CHOB -115
   FAX 202-225-3405
2. Ed Pastor
   CHOB -223
   FAX 202-225-4065
3. Bob Stump
   CHOB -211
   FAX 202-225-6328

Ariz., cont
4. John Shadegg
   CHOB -503
   FAX 202-225-3462
5. Jim Kolbe
   CHOB -205
   FAX 202-225-0378
6. J. D. Hayworth
   LHOB -1023
   FAX 202-225-3263

ARKANSAS
1. Marion Berry
   LHOB -1407
   FAX 202-225-5602
2. Vic Snyder
   LHOB -1319
   FAX 202-225-5903
3. Asa Hutchinson
   LHOB -1535
   FAX
4. Jay Dickey
   CHOB -230
   FAX 202-225-1314

CALIFORNIA
1. Frank Riggs
   LHOB -1714
   FAX 202-225-3403
2. Wally Herger
   RHOB -2433
   FAX 202-225-1609
3. Vic Fazio
   RHOB -2113
   FAX 202-225-0354
4. John T. Doolittle
   LHOB -1526
   FAX 202-225-5444

Calif, cont
5. Robert T. Matsui
   RHOB -2311
   FAX 202-225-0566
6. Lynn Woolsey
   CHOB -439
   FAX 202-225-5163
7. George Miller
   RHOB -2205
   FAX 202-225-5609
8. Nancy Pelosi
   RHOB -2457
   FAX 202-225-8259
9. Ronald V. Dellums
   RHOB -2108
   FAX 202-225-9817
10. Ellen O. Tauscher
    LHOB -1440
    FAX 202-225-5914
11. Richard W., Pombo
    LHOB -1519
    FAX 202-226-0861
12. Tom Lantos
    RHOB -2217
    FAX 202-225-3127
13. Pete Stark
    CHOB -239
    FAX 202-226-3805
14. Anna G. Eshoo
    CHOB -308
    FAX 202-225-8890
15. Tom Campbell
    RHOB -2221
    FAX
16. Zoe Lofgren
    CHOB -118
    FAX 202-225-3336
17. Sam Farr
    LHOB -1117
    FAX 202-225-6791

137

Calif., cont
18. Gary A. Condit
RHOB -2444
FAX 202-225-0819
19. George Radanovich
CHOB -313
FAX 202-225-3402
20. Cal Dooley
LHOB -1227
FAX 202-225-9308
21. Bill Thomas
RHOB 2208
FAX 202-225-8798
22. Walter H. Capps
LHOB -1118
FAX 202-225-5632
23. Elton Gallegly
RHOB -2441
FAX 202-225-1100
24. Brad Sherman
LHOB -1524
FAX 202-225-5879
25. Howard P. McKeon
CHOB -307
FAX 202-226-0683
26. Howard L. Berman
RHOB -2231
FAX 202-225-5279
27. James E. Rogan
CHOB -502
FAX
28. David Dreier
CHOB -411
FAX 202-225-7018
29. Henry A. Waxman
RHOB -2408
FAX 202-225-4099
30. Xavier Becerra
LHOB -1119
FAX 202-225-6235
31. Matthew G. Martinez
RHOB -2239
FAX 202-225-5467
32. Julian C. Dixon
RHOB -2252
FAX 202-225-4091
33. Lucille Roybal-Allard
CHOB -324
FAX 202-226-0350
34. Esteban E. Torres
RHOB -2368
FAX 202-225-9711

Calif., cont
35. Maxine Waters
CHOB -325
FAX 202-225-7854
36. Jane Harman
CHOB -325
FAX 202-225-0684
37. Juanita Millender-
McDonald
FAX
38. Steve Horn
CHOB -129
FAX 202-226-1012
39. Ed Royce
LHOB -1133
FAX 202-225-4111
40. Jerry Lewis
RHOB -2112
FAX 202-225-6498
41. Jay C. Kim
CHOB -435
FAX 202-226-1485
42. George E. Brown, Jr.
RHOB -2300
FAX 202-225-8671
43. Ken Calvert
LHOB -1034
FAX 202-225-2004
44. Sonny Bono
CHOB -512
FAX 202-225-2961
45. Dana Rohrabacher
RHOB -2338
FAX 202-225-0145
46. Loretta Sanchez
LHOB -1529
FAX 202-225-2965
47. Christopher Cox
RHOB -2402
FAX 202-225-9177
48. Ron Packard
RHOB -2162
FAX 202-225-0134
49. Brian P. Bilbray
LHOB -1004
FAX 202-225-2948
50. Bob Filner
CHOB -504
FAX 202-225-9073

Calif., cont
51. Randy Cunningham
CHOB -227
FAX 202-225-2558
52. Duncan Hunger
RHOB -2265
FAX 202-225-0235

COLORADO
1. Diana DeGette
LHOB -1404
FAX 202-225-5657
2. David E. Skaggs
LHOB -1124
FAX 202-225-9127
3. Scott McInnis
CHOB -215
FAX 202-226-0622
4. Bob Schaffer
CHOB -212
FAX 202-225-5870
5. Joel Hefley
RHOB -2351
FAX 202-225-1942
6. Dan Schaefer
RHOB -2353
FAX 202-225-7885

CONNECTICUT
1. Barbara B. Kennelly
CHOB -201
FAX 202-225-1031
2. Sam Gejdenson
RHOB -2416
FAX 202-225-4977
3. Rosa DeLauro
CHOB -436
FAX 202-225-4890
4. Christopher Shays
LHOB -1502
FAX 202-225-9629
5. James H. Maloney
LHOB -1213
FAX 202-225-5746
6. Nancy I. Johnson
CHOB -343
FAX 202-225-4488

DELAWARE
1. Michael N. Castle
LHOB -1207
FAX 202-225-2719

The End of the Rainbow

FLORIDA
1. Joe Scarborough
   LHOB -1523
   FAX 202-225-3414
2. Allen Boyd
   LHOB -1237
   FAX 202-225-5615
3. Corrine Brown
   LHOB -1610
   FAX 202-225-2256
4. Tillie Fowler
   CHOB -413
   FAX 202-225-9318
5. Karen L. Thurman
   CHOB -130
   FAX 202-226-0329
6. Cliff Stearns
   RHOB -2352
   FAX 202-225-3973
7. John L. Mica
   CHOB -336
   FAX 202-226-0821
8. Bill McCollum
   RHOB -2266
   FAX 202-225-0999
9. Michael Bilirakis
   RHOB -2240
   FAX 202-225-4085
10. C. W. Bill Young
    RHOB -2407
    FAX 202-225-9764
11. Jim Davis
    CHOB -327
    FAX 202-225-5652
12. Charles T. Canady
    LHOB -1222
    FAX 202-225-2279
13. Dan Miller
    CHOB -117
    FAX 202-226-0828
14. Porter J. Goss
    CHOB -108
    FAX 202-2256820-
15. Dave Weldon
    CHOB -216
    FAX 202-225-3671
16. Mark Foley
    CHOB -506
    FAX 202-225-3132
17. Carrie P. Meek
    CHOB -404
    FAX 202-226-0777

18. Ileana Ros-Lehtinen
    RHOB -2440
    FAX 202-225-5620
19. Robert Wexler
    LHOB -1609
    FAX 202-225-5974
20. Peter Deutsch
    CHOB -204
    FAX 202-225-8456
21. Lincoln Diaz-Balart
    CHOB -431
    FAX 202-225-8576
22. E. Clay Shaw, Jr
    RHOB -2267
    FAX 202-225-8398
23. Alcee L. Hastings
    LHOB -1039
    FAX 202-226-0690

GEORGIA
1. Jack Kingston
   LHOB -1507
   FAX 202-226-2269
2. Sanford D. Bishop, Jr.
   LHOB -1632
   FAX 202-226-3601
3. Mac Collins
   LHOB -1130
   FAX 202-225-2515
4. John Linder
   LHOB -1318
   FAX 202-225-4696
5. John Lewis
   CHOB -229
   FAX 202-225-0351
6. Newt Gingrich
   RHOB -2428
   FAX 202-225-4656
7. Bob Barr
   LHOB -1607
   FAX 202-225-2944
8. Saxby Chambliss
   LHOB -1708
   FAX 202-225-3013
9. Nathan Deal
   LHOB -1406
   FAX 202-225-8272
10. Charlie Norwood, Jr.
    LHOB -1707
    FAX 202-225-3397

GA., cont
11. Cynthia A. McKinney
    CHOB -124
    FAX 202-226-1605

HAWAII
1. Neil Abercrombie
   LHOB -1233
   FAX 202-225-4580
2. Patsy T. Mink
   RHOB -2135
   FAX 202-225-4987

IDAHO
1. Helen Chenoweth
   LHOB -1722
   FAX 202-225-3029
2. Michael D. Crapo
   CHOB -437
   FAX 202-225-8216

ILLINOIS
1. Bobby L. Rush
   CHOB -131
   FAX 202-226-0333
2. Jesse L. Jackson, Jr.
   CHOB -312
   FAX 202-225-0899
3. William O. Lipinski
   LHOB -1501
   FAX 202-225-1012
4. Luis V. Gutierrez
   CHOB -408
   FAX 202-225-7810
5. Rod R. Blagojevich
   CHOB -501
   FAX 202-225-5603
6. Henry J. Hyde
   RHOB -2110
   FAX 202-225-1166
7. Danny K. Davis
   LHOB -1218
   FAX 202-225-5641
8. Philip M. Crane
   CHOB -233
   FAX 202-225-7830
9. Sidney R. Yates
   RHOB -2109
   FAX 202-225-3493
10. John Edward Porter
    RHOB -2373
    FAX 202-225-0157

ILL. , cont
11. Jerry Weller
LHOB -1710
FAX 202-225-3521
12. Jerry F. Costello
RHOB -2454
FAX 202-225-0285
13. Harris W. Fawell
RHOB -2159
FAX 202-225-9420
14. Dennis Hastert
RHOB -2453
FAX 202-225-0697
15. Thomas W. Ewing
LHOB -1317
FAX 202-225-8071
16. Donald Manzullo
CHOB -426
FAX 202-225-5284
17. Lane Evans
RHOB -2335
FAX 202-225-5396
18. Ray LaHood
CHOB -329
FAX 202-225-9249
19. Glenn Poshard
RHOB -2334
FAX 202-225-1541
20. John M. Shimkus
CHOB -513
FAX 202-225-5880

INDIANA
1. Peter J. Visclosky
RHOB -2464
FAX 202-225-2493
2. David M. McIntosh
LHOB -1208
FAX 202-225-3382
3. Tim Roemer
CHOB -407
FAX 202-225-6798
4. Mark E. Souder
CHOB -508
FAX 202-225-3479
5. Steve Buyer
CHOB -326
FAX 202-225-2267
6. Dan Burton
RHOB -2411
FAX 202-225-0016

IND., cont
7. Edward A. Pease
CHOB -226
FAX
8. John Hostettler
LHOB -1404
FAX 202-225-3284
9. Lee H. Hamilton
RHOB -2314
FAX 202-225-1101
10. Julia M. Carson
LHOB -1541
FAX 202-225-5633

IOWA
1. Jim Leach
RHOB 2186
FAX 202-226-1278
2. Jim Nussle
CHOB -303
FAX 202-225-9129
3. Leunard L. Boswell
LHOB -1029
FAX 202-225-5608
4. Greg Ganske
LHOB -1108
FAX 202-225-3193
5. Tom Latham
CHOB -516
FAX 202-225-3301

KANSAS
1. Jerry Moran
LHOB -1217
FAX 202-225-5124
2. Jim Ryun
CHOB -511
FAX 202-225-7986
3. Vince Snowbarger
CHOB -509
FAX 202-225-5897
4. Todd Tiahrt
LHOB -1319
FAX 202-225-3489

KENTUCKY
1. Edward Whitfield
LHOB -1541
FAX 202-225-3547
2. Ron Lewis
CHOB -412
FAX 202-226-2019

3. Ann Meagher Northup
LHOB -1004
FAX 202-225-5776
4. Jim Bunning
RHOB -2437
FAX 202-225-0003
5. Harold Rogers
RHOB -2468
FAX 202-225-0940
6. Scotty Baesler
CHOB -113
FAX 202-225-2122

LOUISIANA
1. Robert L. Livingston
RHOB -2406
FAX 202-225-0739
2. William J. Jefferson
CHOB -240
FAX 202-225-1988
3. W.J. "Billy" Tauzin
RHOB -2183
FAX 202-225-0563
4. Jim McCrery
CHOB -225
FAX 202-225-8039
5. John Cooksey
CHOB -317
FAX 202-225-5639
6. Richard H. Baker
CHOB -434
FAX 202-225-7313
7. Chris John
LHOB -1504
FAX 202-225-5724

MAINE
1. Thomas H. Allen
LHOB -1630
FAX 202-225-5590
2. John Baldacci
LHOB -1740
FAX 202-225-2943

MARYLAND
1. Wayne T. Gilchrest
CHOB -332
FAX 202-225-0254
2. Robert Ehrlich, Jr.
CHOB -315
FAX 202-225-3094

The End of the Rainbow

Maryland, cont
3. Benjamin L. Cardin
   CHOB -104
   FAX 202-225-9219
4. Albert R. Wynn
   CHOB -418
   FAX 202-225-8714
5. Steny H. Hoyer
   LHOB -1705 FAX
   FAX 202-225-4300
6. Roscoe G. Bartlett
   CHOB -322
   FAX 202-225-2193
7. Elijah E. Cummings
   RHOB -2419
   FAX 202-225-3178
8. Constance A. Morella
   CHOB -106
   FAX 202-225-1389

MASSACHUSETTS
1. John W. Olver
   LHOB -1027
   FAX 202-226-1224
2. Richard E. Neal
   RHOB -2431
   FAX 202-225-8112
3. James P. McGovern
   CHOB -2210
   FAX 202-225-5759
4. Barney Frank
   RHOB -2210
   FAX 202-225-0182
5. Martin Meehan
   CHOB -318
   FAX 202-226-0771
6. John F. Tierney
   CHOB -120
   FAX 202-225-5915
7. Edward Markey
   RHOB -2133
   FAX 202-225-1716
8. Joseph P. Kennedy II
   RHOB -2242
   FAX 202-225-9322
9. Joe Moakley
   CHOB -235
   FAX 202-225-3984
10. Wm. D. Delahunt
    LHOB -1517
    FAX 202-225-3111

MICHIGAN
1. Bart Stupak
   CHOB -317
   FAX 202-225-4744
2. Peter Hoekstra
   LHOB -1122
   FAX 202-226-0779
3. Vernon J. Ehlers
   LHOB 1717
   FAX 202-225-5144
4. Dave Camp
   CHOB -137
   FAX 202-225-9679
5. James A. Barcia
   LHOB -1410
   FAX 202-225-2168
6. Fred Upton
   RHOB -2333
   FAX 202-225-4986
7. Nick Smith
   LHOB -1530
   FAX 202-225-6281
8. Debbie Stabenow
   LHOB 1516
   FAX 202-225-5820
9. Dale E. Kildee
   RHOB 2187
   FAX 202-225-6393
10. David E. Bonior
    RHOB -2207
    FAX 202-226-1169
11. Joe Knollenberg
    LHOB -1221
    FAX 202-226-2356
12. Sander M. Levin
    RHOB -2230
    FAX 202-226-1033
13. Lynn N. Rivers
    LHOB -1116
    FAX 202-225-3404
14. John Conyers, Jr.
    RHOB -2426
    FAX 202-225-0072
15. Carolynb Cheeks
        Kilpatrick
    CHOB -503
    FAX 202-225-5730
16. John D. Dingell
    RHOB -2328
    FAX 202-225-7426

MINNESOTA
1. Gil Gutknecht
   CHOB -425
   FAX 202-225-3246
2. David Minge
   LHOB -1415
   FAX 202-226-0836
3. Jim Ramstad
   CHOB -103
   FAX 202-225-6351
4. Bruce F. Vento
   RHOB -2304
   FAX 202-225-1968
5. Martin Olav Sabo
   RHOB -2336
   FAX 202-225-4886
6. Wm. P. Luther
   LHOB -1419
   FAX 202-225-3368
7. Collin C. Peterson
   LHOB -1314
   FAX 202-225-1593
8. James L. Oberstar
   RHOB -2366
   FAX 202-225-0699

MISSISSIPPI
1. Roger F. Wicker
   CHOB -206
   FAX 202-225-3549
2. Bennie G. Thompson
   LHOB -1408
   FAX 202-225-5898
3. Charles W. Pickering
   CHOB -427
   FAX 202-225-5797
4. Mike Parker
   RHOB -2445
   FAX 202-225-5886
5. Gene Taylor
   RHOB -2447
   FAX 202-225-7074

MISSOURI
1. Wm. Clay
   RHOB -2306
   FAX 202-225-1725
2. James M. Talent
   LHOB -1022
   FAX 202-225-2563
3. Richard A. Gephardt
   LHOB -1226
   FAX 202-225-7452

MO., cont
4. Ike Skelton
RHOB -2227
FAX 202-225-2695
5. Karen McCarthy
LHOB -1232
FAX 202-225-4403
6. Pat Danner
LHOB -1323
FAX 202-225-8221
7. Roy Blunt
CHOB -508
FAX 202-225-5604
8. Jo Ann Emerson
CHOB -132
FAX
9. Kenny Hulshof
LHOB -1728
FAX 202-225-5712

MONTANA
1. Rick Hill
LHOB -1037
FAX 202-225-5687

NEBRASKA
1. Doug Bereuter
RHOB -2348
FAX 202-226-1148
2. Jon Christensen
LHOB -1020
FAX 202-225-3032
3. Bill Barrett
LHOB 1213
FAX 202-225-0207

NEVADA
1. John E. Ensign
CHOB -414
FAX 202-225-3119
2. Jim Gibbons
LHOB -1116
FAX 202-225-5679

NEW HAMPSHIRE
1. John Sununu
LHOB -1229
FAX 202-225-5822
2. Charles F. Bass
LHOB -1728
FAX 202-225-2946

NEW JERSEY
1. Robert E. Andrews
RHOB -2439
FAX 202-225-6583
2. Frank A. LoBiondo
CHOB -513
FAX 202-225-3318
3. Jim Saxton
CHOB -339
FAX 202-225-0778
4. Christopher H. Smith
RHOB -2370
FAX 202-225-7768
5. Marge Roukema
RHOB 2469
FAX 202-225-9048
6. Frank Pallone, Jr.
CHOB 420
FAX 202-225-9665
7. Bob Franks
CHOB -429
FAX 202-225-9460
8. Wm. J. Pascrell, Jr.
LHOB -1722
FAX 202-225-5782
9. Steven R. Rothman
LHOB -1607
FAX 202-225-5851
10. Donald M. Payne
RHOB -2244
FAX 202-225-4160
11. Rodney P. Frelinghuysen
CHOB -514
FAX 202-225-3186
12. Mike Pappas
LHOB -1710
FAX 202-225-6025
13. Robert Menendez
LHOB -1730
FAX 202-226-0792

NEW MEXICO
1. Stephen Schiff
RHOB -2404
FAX 202-225-4975
2. Joe Skeen
RHOB -2367
FAX 202-225-9599
3. Bill Richardson
RHOB -2209
FAX 202-225-1950

NEW YORK
1. Michael Forbes
CHOB -502
FAX 202-225-3143
2. Rick Lazio
CHOB -314
FAX 202-225-4669
3. Peter T. King
CHOB -224
FAX 202-226-2279
4. Carolyn McCarthy
LHOB -1725
FAX 202-225-5758
5. Gary L. Ackerman
RHOB -2243
FAX 202-225-1589
6. Floyd H. Flake
LHOB -1035
FAX 202-226-4169
7. Thomas J. Manton
RHOB -2235
FAX 202-225-1909
8. Jerrold Nadler
CHOB -109
FAX 202-225-6923
9. Charles E. Schumer
RHOB -2211
FAX 202-225-4183
10. Edolphus Towns
RHOB -2232
FAX 202-225-1018
11. Major R. Owens
RHOB -2305
FAX 202-226-0112
12. Nydia M. Valazquez
CHOB -132
FAX 202-226-0327
13. Susan Molinari
RHOB -2435
FAX 202-226-1272
14. Carolyn B. Maloney
LHOB -1504
FAX 202-225-4709
15. Charles B. Rangel
RHOB -2354
FAX 202-225-0816
16. Jose' E. Serrano
RHOB -2342
FAX 202-225-6001
17. Eliot L. Engel
LHOB -1433
FAX 202-225-5513

The End of the Rainbow

NY, cont
18. Nita M. Lowey
    RHOB -2421
    FAX 202-225-0546
19. Sue W. Kelly
    LHOB -1037
    FAX 202-225-3289
20. Benjamin A. Gilman
    RHOB -2449
    FAX 202-225-2541
21. Michael R. McNulty
    RHOB -2442
    FAX 202-225-5077
22. Gerald Solomon
    RHOB 2206
    FAX 202-225-6234
23. Sherwood Boehlert
    RHOB -2246
    FAX 202-225-1891
24. John M. McHugh
    CHOB -416
    FAX 202-226-0621
25. James T. Walsh
    LHOB -1330
    FAX 202-225-4042
26. Maurice Hinchey
    LHOB -1524
    FAX 202-226-0774
27. Bill Paxon
    RHOB -2436
    FAX 202-225-5910
28. Louise Slaughter
    RHOB -2347
    FAX 202-225-7822
29. John LaFalce
    RHOB -2310
    FAX 202-225-8693
30. Jack Quinn
    CHOB -331
    FAX 202-226-0347
31. Amo Houghton
    LHOB -1110
    FAX 202-225-5574

NORTH CAROLINA
1. Eva M. Clayton
    CHOB -222
    FAX 202-225-3354
2. Bob Etheridge
    LHOB -1641
    FAX 202-225-5662

N. Car., cont
3. Walter B. Jones, Jr.
    CHOB -214
    FAX 202-225-3286
4. David E. Price
    RHOB -2162
    FAX 202-225-2014
5. Richard Burr
    LHOB -1431
    FAX 202-225-2995
6. Howard Coble
    CHOB -403
    FAX 202-225-8611
7. Mike McIntyre
    LHOB -1605
    FAX 202-225-5773
8. W. G. Hefner
    RHOB -2470
    FAX 202-225-4036
9. Sue Myrick
    CHOB -509
    FAX 202-225-3389
10. Cass Ballenger
    RHOB 2238
    FAX 202-225-0316
11. Charles H. Taylor
    CHOB -231
    FAX 202-226-6405
12. Melvin L. Watt
    LHOB -1230
    FAX 202-225-1512

NORTH DAKOTA
1. Earl Pomeroy
    LHOB -1533
    FAX 202-226-0893

OHIO
1. Steven J. Chabot
    LHOB -1641
    FAX 202-225-3012
2. Rob Portman
    CHOB -238
    FAX 202-225-1992
3. Tony P. Hall
    LHOB -1432
    FAX 202-225-6766
4. Michael G. Oxley
    RHOB -2233
    FAX 202-226-1160
5. Paul E. Gillmor
    LHOB -1203
    FAX 202-225-1985

Ohio, cont
6. Ted Strickland
    CHOB -336
    FAX 202-225-5907
7. David L. Hobson
    LHOB -1514
    FAX 202-225-1984
8. John A. Boehner
    LHOB -1011
    FAX 202-225-0704
9. Marcy Kaptur
    RHOB -2104
    FAX 202-225-7711
10. Dennis J. Kucinich
    LHOB -1730
    FAX
11. Louis Stokes
    RHOB -2365
    FAX 202-225-1339
12. John R. Kasich
    LHOB -1131
    FAX 202-226-5483
13. Sherrod Brown
    LHOB -1019
    FAX 202-225-2266
14. Thomas C. Sawyer
    LHOB -1414
    FAX 202-225-5278
15. Deborah Pryce
    CHOB -221
    FAX 202-226-0309
16. Ralph Regula
    RHOB -2309
    FAX 202-225-3059
17. James Traficant, Jr.
    RHOB -2446
    FAX 202-225-3719
18. Robert W. Ney
    LHOB -1605
    FAX 202-225-3394
19. Steve C. LaTourette
    LHOB 1508
    FAX 202-225-3307

OKLAHOMA
1. Steve Largent
    CHOB -410
    FAX 202-225-9187
2. Tom A. Coburn
    CHOB -511
    FAX 202-225-3038

143

Okla., cont
3. Wes Watkins
   RHOB -2312
FAX 202-225-5966
4. J. C. Watts, Jr.
   LHOB -1713
FAX 202-225-3512
5. Ernest J. Istook, Jr.
   CHOB -119
FAX 202-226-1463
6. Frank D. Lucas
   CHOB -107
FAX 202-225-8698

OREGON
1. Elizabeth Furse
   CHOB -316
FAX 202-225-9497
2. Robert F. Smith
   LHOB -1126
FAX 202-225-5774
3. Earl Blumenauer
   LHOB -1111
FAX 202-225-8941
4. Peter A. DeFazio
   RHOB -2143
FAX 202-225-0373
5. Darlene Hooley
   LHOB 1419
FAX 202-225-5699

PENNSYLVANIA
1. Thomas Foglietta
   CHOB -341
FAX 202-225-0088
2. Chaka Fattah
   LHOB -1205
FAX 202-225-3127
3. Robert A. Borski
   RHOB -2182
FAX 202-225-4628
4. Ron Klink
   CHOB -125
FAX 202-226-2274
5. John E. Peterson
   LHOB -1020
FAX 202-225-5796
6. Tim Holden
   LHOB -1421
FAX 202-226-0996
7. Curt Weldon
   RHOB -2452
FAX 202-225-8137

PA., cont
8. James Greenwood
   CHOB -430
FAX 202-225-9511
9. Bud Shuster
   RHOB -2188
FAX 202-225-2486
10. Joseph M. McDade
    RHOB -2107
FAX 202-225-9594
11. Paul E. Kanjorski
    RHOB -2429
FAX 202-225-9024
12. John P. Murtha
    RHOB -2423
FAX 202-225-5709
13. Jon D. Fox
    CHOB -510
FAX 202-225-3155
14. William J. Coyne
    RHOB -2455
FAX 202-225-1844
15. Paul McHale
    CHOB -217
FAX 202-225-5320
16. Joseph R. Pitts
    CHOB -504
FAX
17. George W. Gekas
    RHOB -2410
FAX 202-225-8440
18. Michael F. Doyle
    LHOB -1218
FAX 202-225-3084
19. William F. Goodling
    RHOB 2263
FAX 202-226-1000
20. Frank Mascara
    LHOB 1531
FAX 202-225-3377
21. Phil English
    LHOB 1721
FAX 202-225-3103

RHODE ISLAND
1. Patrick J. Kennedy
   LHOB -1505
FAX 202-225-3290
2. Robert A. Weygand
   CHOB -507
FAX 202-225-5976

SOUTH CAROLINA
1. Mark Sanford
   LHOB -1223
FAX 202-225-3407
2. Floyd Spence
   RHOB 2405
FAX 202-225-2455
3. Lindsey O. Graham
   LHOB 1429
FAX 202-225-3216
4. Bob Inglis
   LHOB -1237
FAX 202-226-1177
5. John M. Spratt, Jr.
   LHOB -1536
FAX 202-225-0464
6. James E. Clyburn
   CHOB -319
FAX 202-225-2313

SOUTH DAKOTA
1. John R. Thune
   CHOB -506
FAX 202-225-5823

TENNESSEE
1. William L. Jenkins
   LHOB -1708
FAX 202-225-5714
2. John J. Kuncan, Jr.
   RHOB -2400
FAX 202-225-6440
3. Zach Wamp
   CHOB -423
FAX 202-225-3494
4. Van Hilleary
   CHOB -114
FAX 202-225-3272
5. Bob Clement
   RHOB -2229
FAX 202-226-1035
6. Bart Gordon
   RHOB -2201
FAX 202-225-6887
7. Ed Bryant
   LHOB -1516
FAX 202-225-2989
8. John S. Tanner
   LHOB -1127
FAX 202-225-1765
9. Harold E. Ford, Jr.
   LHOB -1523
FAX 202-225-5663

The End of the Rainbow

TEXAS
1. Max Sandlin
   CHOB -214
   FAX 202-225-5866
2. Jim Turner
   LHOB -1508
   FAX 202-225-5955
3. Sam Johnson
   LHOB -1030
   FAX 202-225-1485
4. Ralph M. Hall
   RHOB -2236
   FAX 202-225-3332
5. Pete Sessions
   LHOB -1318
   FAX 202-225-0327
6. Joe Barton
   RHOB -2264
   FAX 202-225-3052
7. Bill Archer
   LHOB -1236
   FAX 202-225-4831
8. Kevin Brady
   LHOB -1531
   FAX 202-225-5524
9. Nick Lampson
   CHOB -417
   FAX
10. Lloyd Doggett
    CHOB -126
    FAX 202-225-3073
11. Chet Edwards
    CHOB -328
    FAX 202-225-0350
12. Kay Granger
    CHOB -515
    FAX
13. Wm. M. Thornberry
    LHOB -1535
    FAX 202-225-3486
14. Ron Paul
    CHOB -203
    FAX
15. Ruben Hinojosa
    LHOB -1032
    FAX 202-225-5688
16 Silvestre Reyes
    CHOB -514
    FAX 202-225-2016
17. Charles W. Stenholm
    LHOB -1211
    FAX 202-225-2234

Texas, cont
18. Sheila Jackson-Lee
    LHOB -1520
    FAX 202-225-3317
19. Larry Combest
    LHOB -1511
    FAX 202-225-9615
20. Henry B. Gonzalez
    RHOB -2413
    FAX 202-225-1915
21. Lamar S., Smith
    RHOB 2443
    FAX 202-225-8628
22. Tom DeLay
    CHOB -203
    FAX 202-225-5241
23. Henry Bonilla
    LHOB -1427
    FAX 202-225-2237
24. Martin Frost
    RHOB 2459
    FAX 202-225-4951
25. Ken Bentsen
    CHOB -128
    FAX 202-225-2947
26. Richard K. Armey
    CHOB -301
    FAX 202-226-8100
27. Solomon P. Ortiz
    RHOB 2136
    FAX 202-226-1134
28. Frank Tejeda
    CHOB -323
    FAX 202-225-1641
29. Gene Green
    LHOB -1024
    FAX 202-225-9903
30. Eddie B. Johnson
    LHOB -1123
    FAX 202-226-1477

UTAH
1. James V. Hansen
   RHOB -2466
   FAX 202-225-5857
2. Merrill Cook
   LHOB -1431
   FAX 202-225-5638
3. Christopher B. Cannon
   CHOB -118
   FAX 202-225-5629

VERMONT
1. Bernard Sanders
   CHOB -213
   FAX 202-225-6790

VIRGINIA
1. Herbert H. Bateman
   RHOB -2350
   FAX 202-225-4382
2. Owen B., Pickett
   RHOB -2430
   FAX 202-225-4218
3. Robert C. Scott
   CHOB -501
   FAX 202-225-8354
4. Norman Sisisky
   RHOB -2371
   FAX 202-226-1170
5. Virgil H. Goode, Jr.
   LHOB -1520
   FAX 202-225-5681
6. Bob Goodlatte
   CHOB -123
   FAX 202-225-9681
7. Thomas J. Bliley, Jr.
   RHOB -2241
   FAX 202-225-0011
8. Jame P. Moran
   CHOB 405
   FAX 202-225-0017
9. Rick Boucher
   RHOB -2245
   FAX 202-225-0442
10. Frank R. Wolf
    CHOB -241
    FAX 202-225-0437
11. Thomas M. Davis
    CHOB -415
    FAX 202-225-3071

WASHINGTON
1. Rick White
   CHOB -116
   FAX 202-225-3524
2. Jack Metcalf
   CHOB 507
   FAX 202-225-4420
3. Linda Smith
   LHOB -1217
   FAX 202-225-3478
4. Richard Hastings
   LHOB -1229
   FAX 202-225-3251

Wash, cont
5. George Nethercutt
   LHOB -1527
   FAX 202-225-3392
6. Norman D. Dicks
   RHOB -2467
   FAX 202-226-1176
7. Jim McDermott
   RHOB -2349
   FAX 202-225-9212
8. Jennifer Dunn
   CHOB -432
   FAX 202-225-8673
9. Adam Smith
   LHOB -1505
   FAX 202-225-5893

WEST VIRGINIA
1. Alan B. Mollohan
   RHOB -2427
   FAX 202-225-7564
2. Robert E. Wise, Jr.
   RHOB -2434
   FAX 202-225-7856
3. Nick J. Rahall, II
   RHOB -2269
   FAX 202-225-9061

WISCONSIN
1. Mark W. Neumann
   LHOB -1725
   FAX 202-225-3393
2. Scott L. Klug
   LHOB -1113
   FAX 202-225-6942
3. Ron Kind
   LHOB -1713
   FAX 202-225-5739
4. Gerald D. Kleczka
   RHOB -2301
   FAX 202-225-8135
5. Thomas M. Barrett
   LHOB -1224
   FAX 202-225-3571
6. Thomas E. Petri
   RHOB -2262
   FAX 202-225-2356
7. David R. Obey
   RHOB -2462
   FAX
8. Jay Johnson
   LHOB -1313
   FAX 202-225-5729
9. F. J. Sensenbrenner, Jr.
   RHOB -2332
   FAX 202-225-3190

WYOMING
1. Barbara Cubin
   LHOB -1114
   FAX 202-225-3057

146

Additional books may be ordered
by sending $ 12.50 (check or money order)

CPA Books
404 E. Ludlow
Rolling Prairie, IN 46371

Send Check or Money Order ($12.50 each)
(includes taxes, shipping and handling.)

Be sure to include: (please print)

....

Name_____

Shipping Address_____

_____

City_____ State_____ Zip_____